Early Childhood Writing Centers

Early Childhood Writing Centers

JUDY HERR   YVONNE LIBBY

HARCOURT BRACE COLLEGE PUBLISHERS

Fort Worth   Philadelphia   San Diego   New York   Orlando   Austin   San Antonio
Toronto   Montreal   London   Sydney   Tokyo

PUBLISHER	Ted Buchholz
ACQUISITIONS EDITOR	Jo-Anne Weaver
PROJECT EDITOR	Laura Hanna
PRODUCTION MANAGER	Cynthia Young
BOOK DESIGNER	Peggy Young

Chapter Opener Illustrations by Bill Alger, Dallas, TX.

Address Editorial Correspondence To:
Harcourt Brace College Publishers, 301 Commerce Street,
Suite 3700, Fort Worth, TX 76102

Address Orders To:
Harcourt Brace & Company, 6277 Sea Harbor Drive,
Orlando, FL 32887
1-800-782-4479, or 1-800-433-0001 (in Florida)

Printed in the United States of America
Library of Congress Catalogue Number: 92-75552
ISBN: 0-15-500482-4
4 5 6 7 8 9 0 1 2 3 069 9 8 7 6 5 4 3 2 1

PREFACE

Early Childhood Writing Centers contains ideas, instructions, and illustrative photographs of materials prepared by teachers to promote physical, social, and cognitive growth of young children. Like those of our previous publications, these educational materials have been designed to encourage curiosity and initiative through active exploration and interaction with other children and adults. Such interaction should produce meaningful developmental learning experiences for young children. Learning in young children occurs as a result of the interaction between his/her thoughts and experiences with materials and ideas.

The creative, teacher-made materials in this book have been successfully used in children's programs in the Child and Family Study Center at the University of Wisconsin–Stout, as well as in kindergarten programs. Primarily the materials were placed in the writing centers and made available for children to explore and manipulate during large blocks of time referred to as *center time*. Other educational programs may refer to this time as self-selected, small group, or play time. Many of the materials offer the children a choice of solitary activity or can be used in a small group.

The writing center is an important classroom area for early childhood programs. It contains individualized learning materials for developing basic skills. Activities placed in this location can promote the children's growth in a number of developmental areas. Among them are:

- the development of visual discrimination skills
- the development of eye–hand coordination skills
- the recognition of alphabet letters and numerals
- practice forming alphabet letters and numerals
- the development of an appreciation for and interest in the printed word
- the development of language skills

This book represents ideas that have been gleaned from our experiences teaching young children and educating teachers of young children in a university setting. While it is impossible to recognize all of the individuals who have encouraged us to share our ideas, we would be remiss in failing to acknowledge the following: Carla Ahmann, Mary Arnevik, Mary Babula, Katie Bettner, Terry Bloomberg, Margaret Brunn, Bruce Cunningham, Linda DeMoe, Rita Pittman Devery, Esther Fahm, Judy Gifford, Jodi Gould, Nancy Gowan, Nancy Graese, Sue Herbach, Patti Herman, Joan Herwig, Carol Hillmer, Priscilla Huffman, Paula Iverson, Candy Jordon, Angela LaBonne Kaiser, Betz Kaster, Kelly Kuester, Beth Libby, Patti Lightfield, Diane Long, Janet Maffet, Ginny McCaig,

Nancy McCarthy, Cindy Merdc, Betty Misselt, Teresa Mitchell, Donna Muenich, Robin Muza, Carole Nelson, Wendy Nielson, Paula Noll, Nan Olson, Cari Parent, Steve Petznick, Lori Singerhouse Register, Peg Saienga, Kathy Rucker Schaeffer, Cheryl Smith, Sue Springer, Karen Stephens, Paul Tennyson, Lori Wayne, Mary Eileen Zenk, and Karen Zimmerman.

TABLE OF CONTENTS

I N T R O D U C T I O N

The materials included in *Early Childhood Writing Centers* have been designed to promote children's writing skills. The book contains a variety of manipulative activities, ranging from simple to complex, that encourage exploration and discovery. This information should be helpful in assisting you to develop and implement a writing center in your classroom.

Learning Center Definition

A learning center is a classroom area that contains a collection of related materials and activities. Centers that are often developed and introduced in early childhood settings are in art, math, music, science, social studies, language arts, library, and writing.

The Role of the Teacher

Your role as a teacher is multifaceted. It includes observing, preparing, introducing the center and material, encouraging children to participate at their own developmental level, and evaluating the materials and individual children's progress. To illustrate: First you will assess the developmental needs and interests of the children in your classroom. Once this task is completed, you can design and prepare developmentally appropriate materials. As each new piece of teacher-made material is added to the center, you should introduce it to the children. You can do this in one of two ways. You can demonstrate the skill to individual children at a group time, if developmentally appropriate. After introducing the material, you can encourage the children to independently explore it. Then, too, you provide the children feedback on their progress.

Finally, you can evaluate the children's progress and the effectiveness of the materials. If needed, materials can be adapted to the skill level of the children and/or to the classroom curriculum theme.

Teaching Strategies

Teachers can use several strategies for encouraging the children to become involved in the writing center. Among them are:

1. Asking questions, such as, "What is new in the writing center today?"
2. Posting some of the children's finished products on a bulletin board. This can be an open bulletin board labeled ANNOUNCEMENTS or OUR WORK.
3. Adding new materials to the center on a continuous basis to create interest and adapt to the children's skill level.

4. Providing supplies for the children to create their own learning materials, such as paper, writing tools, chalkboard, and computers.

5. Providing opportunities for the children to share with others the work they created in the center.

6. Rotating materials periodically so that their effectiveness is not lost.

7. Providing immediate reinforcement and/or encouragement after a child completes a project or task.

Material Organization

Descriptions for each teaching aid in this book include four components: (1) children's developmental goals, (2) related curriculum themes, (3) tools and accessories, and (4) variations and extensions.

Developmental Goals

The developmental goals are listed for every piece of teacher-made material. These goals address the material's value by describing how the children's growth and development can be promoted. For example, by tracing alphabet stencils the children may learn:

- to recognize letters of the alphabet
- to develop eye–hand coordination skills
- to develop small-muscle skills
- to develop visual perceptual skills
- to develop an appreciation of the printed word
- to develop problem-solving skills

Related Curriculum Themes

Themes are general ideas or concepts to which various materials relate. Possible curriculum themes have been included, although the teacher-made materials described in this book could be adapted to the classroom curriculum theme. A variety of concepts can usually be developed with any teacher-made material. Themes listed in the activity description are:

Curriculum Themes

Airport	Baking	Breads
Alphabet Letters	Baskets	Breakfast Foods
Animal Friends	Big/Little	Brushes
Apples	Birds	Buildings
Art	Birthdays	Bulbs
Babies	Books	Camping

Weather	Winter	Writing Tools
We Create	Words	Zoo Animals
Wheels	Writing	
Wild Animals	Writing Surfaces	

Directions

This section outlines the steps in preparing each material. To save time, there are two practices that you will want to follow. First, study the photography in the book. Then collect all of the tools and materials that are needed to construct the teaching aid.

Tools and Accessories

A list of possible accessories for each teacher-made material is also included. Among them are watercolor markers, crayons, grease pencils, damp cloth, and sponge. Feel free to add additional supplies for the children's use.

Variations and Extensions

There are usually many ways to vary or extend materials made for children's use. Ideas have been outlined to simplify or make the material more challenging.

Using the Materials

To plan a developmentally appropriate early childhood curriculum, you need to begin with a basic knowledge of how children grow, develop, and learn. Child development theory will help you understand children's approach to learning how to write. Familiarity with developmental theory will also assist you in planning developmentally appropriate materials and activities.

In selecting or adapting activities, there are several factors to consider:

1. The needs and interests of your children. Select materials that will stimulate the children's curiosity. Typically you will find that four-, five-, six-, and seven-year-old children will appear the most enthusiastic about the writing center materials. Most three-year-old children and some four year olds lack the prerequisite skills for writing activities. Typically, children of this age are more interested in painting and drawing. These skills are necessary to provide the children practice in the small-muscle and eye–hand coordination skills that are prerequisites for writing.

2. Select or design materials that build on the children's previous experiences. If you have taken your class to visit a local bakery, build on that experience. Add materials related to the bakery to the writing center. You could have the children dictate a story about their trip to the bakery. Across a sheet of large tagboard or writing paper, print the title THE BAKERY. As the children dictate the words, print their recollections of the trip. When you finish, hang the chart in the writing center. You could also make a chart

of vocabulary words related to the bakery. As you study this book, your ideas for writing center materials will increase. As a result, you will easily be able to adapt interesting materials that the children will enjoy exploring, and thus, develop an enjoyment of the writing process.

Supplies to Save

Construction of teacher-made materials will be easier if you make it a habit to collect supplies on an ongoing basis. To do this, parents of the children in your class could be contacted to save materials. Begin by sending home a letter, or post a note on the parents' bulletin board. Be specific. Tell them the materials that would be the most beneficial. You may be pleasantly surprised at their response. Possible supplies to save:

Paper	Boxes	Magazines
Calendar Pictures	Catalogs	Fabric
Gift Wrapping Paper	Wallpaper Books	Stationery
Buttons	Envelopes	Stickers
Pencils	Greeting Cards	Book covers
Folders	Newspapers	Rubber Stamps
Egg Cartons	Library Pocket Cards	Berry Baskets
Tongue Depressors	Styrofoam Trays	Cube Boxes
Photographs	Stationery Boxes	Felt Pieces

Writing Tools

Children enjoy using a variety of writing tools. You may find that you can create interest by introducing new tools on a periodic basis. Suggestions for these include:

Chalk	Colored Pens
Crayons	Grease Pencils
Felt-tip Markers: fine, medium, and broad widths	Oil Pastels
Pencils: colored, lead	

Your children can write with permanent broad-tip markers directly on a laminated piece of material. (Interestingly, these markings can be removed by applying hair spray and wiping immediately.)

Within a given classroom, there is usually a wide range of children's developmental abilities. By using the markers, you can tailor the material to make it developmentally appropriate. For example, a game board could be constructed of tagboard and laminated. Then the lettering could be printed on the lamination. This would provide you with the flexibility needed to adapt the material. Shapes could be used for most three year olds, for example, and letters for many four and five year olds.

Writing Surfaces

Just as children enjoy using a variety of writing tools, they like using a variety of writing surfaces. Many of these writing surfaces can be obtained at little or no expense.

Examples include:

Newsprint	Index Cards
Computer Paper	Sandpaper
Construction Paper (fade resistant)	Cardboard Boxes
Gift Wrapping Paper	Shirt Boxes
Chalkboards	Tagboard Sheets: colored and white
Audiovisual Boards	

Adhesives

Several types of adhesives are effective for preparing teacher-made materials. Included are paste, *regular* glue, *hot* glue, and rubber cement. Paste is the least expensive adhesive source; it is not always desirable. You may experience difficulty in spreading thin, even coats. Then, too, you may find that when the paste dries, the edges of the material curl. When used by the children, the curled edges may tear, resulting in either a damaged or unattractive piece of material.

Glue. An alternative is glue. It is more effective than paste. However, it is also more expensive. This prohibits many teachers and schools with restricted budgets from utilizing the product.

Hot-Glue Gun. You may be asking yourself, "How effective is a hot-glue gun?" This tool may be effectively used in constructing materials from wood and plastic. It is not necessary, however, for constructing materials described in this book.

Rubber Cement. Rubber cement is readily available at school supply, office supply, and discount stores. This adhesive is most effective when working with paper and tagboard, the supplies often utilized in preparing materials included in this book. One caution: This product should be used in a well-ventilated area as it produces an unpleasant odor.

Lettering

Prior to the preparation of materials, practice manuscript writing to ensure that it appears professional. You may feel more comfortable using a soft-lead pencil to first sketch your letters. Once satisfied with your letter formation, trace over the letter using a medium felt-tip marker.

Lettering. Lettering should be in proportion to the size of the objects pictured. Chapter 11 contains two sizes of uppercase and lowercase manuscript letters. You may find it helpful to cut out these letters and trace them on heavy tagboard so that they can be used as patterns when preparing materials. The letters can be enlarged or reduced in size by using an opaque projector or some types of copy machines.

Titles. The title should be used to describe the teaching material. The color used to create the title should complement the background paper, as well as objects pictured. Titles need to be created from strong colors and provide contrast. As a result, you will find that primary colors make interesting titles.

You may question the type of lettering—uppercase or lowercase—that should be used in preparing titles. Some teachers prefer to use uppercase letters when the title is not a complete sentence. For a complete sentence, they prefer capitalizing the first word. Also, they place a period at the end of the sentence.

Examples include:

INCOMPLETE SENTENCES	COMPLETE SENTENCES
Writing	Draw your home.
My home	You can write.
A truck	Select a gift.
Water animals	Write your name.
Our world	Choose a color.
Valentine's Day	Find the letters.

Making Materials

Whether you prepare the teacher materials illustrated in this book or design your own, using the following suggestions will be helpful:

1. Select a large clean area to prepare your materials.

2. Collect supplies, including a tool set. Include items such as:

Ruler, Yardstick, and/or Straightedge

Scissors

Soft-Lead Pencils

Glue, Rubber Cement, and/or Paste

Colored Felt-tip Markers

CRAY-PAS

Colored Pencils

---

3. Prepare sets of uppercase and lowercase letters that are located in Chapter 11 of this book. Adapt the size to your classroom bulletin board and standard chart paper.

Selecting Coloring Media

A key to professional appearing materials is to have evenly applied color. To apply color evenly, care must be taken in choosing the appropriate medium. There are several types that can be successfully used. CRAY-PAS and watercolor markers are the most effective. Although crayons can be used, teachers generally prefer the finished appearance of CRAY-PAS and markers.

CRAY-PAS. CRAY-PAS usually produce a smoother image than crayons. CRAY-PAS are oil-based coloring tools that can be purchased from an art supply store, exhibits at professional conferences, and through school supply catalogs.

Unlike the felt-tip marker, the most effective method of applying color with CRAY-PAS is by making a horizontal sweeping motion. To do this, begin by removing the paper wrapper that identifies the name of the color. Then pick up a CRAY-PAS by placing your thumb and forefinger on the center of the writing tool. By holding it in this position, a more uniform distribution of color is generally produced.

After completing the color application, use a paper tissue to rub, and thereby evenly distribute, the color. In order to prevent mixing colors, use a separate tissue for each color.

Watercolor Marker. Felt-tip markers can also be purchased at novelty, school supply or other stores that market stationery supplies. The most effective markers are those with a wide felt tip. To apply the color, draw vertical lines in one direction. For example, when filling in color on a square box, begin at the upper left corner. Draw a line straight down from the top. Carefully remove the marker from the paper. Then move the marker to the top of the box again. Carefully align the tip of the marker adjacent to the first line. Position the marker so there is no overlap of lines. Continue repeating this procedure until the entire box is covered with color.

Preparing Patterns

The patterns used for the figures on teaching materials in this book may be prepared in several ways. You may have the artistic skill to draw them free-hand. Otherwise, you can choose patterns from coloring books or children's storybooks. By placing these materials under an opaque or overhead projector, you can trace the designs and enlarge them if necessary.

Opaque Projector. The opaque projector is an excellent tool for people who are not skilled at drawing. To use this piece of equipment, place the picture that needs to be magnified on the tray. Then tape a piece of tagboard or construction paper onto a wall or door. Adjust the machine to obtain the figure size that is in proportion to your paper, bulletin or chart, and other figures. Using a pencil, lightly trace the image onto the paper. If color is needed, it is easier to fill it in on a flat surface, such as a table or desk, after reproducing the object.

Overhead Projector. Place a transparency of the figure on the glass plate. After this, tape a piece of tagboard, construction or other type of paper on the wall. Turn the lamp on using the switch in front of the projector. Adjust the size of the figure by moving the projector. For smaller figures, move the projector closer to the paper. For larger figures, move the projector farther away from the paper.

Evaluating Materials

CRITERIA FOR WRITING CENTER MATERIALS

	Commendable	Acceptable	Needs Improvement
1. Are the teaching criteria clear?			
2. Does the piece of teacher-made material enrich the activities in the writing center?			
3. Does the material motivate action and stimulate curiosity?			
4. Does the material help develop a skill?			
5. Is the material relevant, projecting accurate and up-to-date concepts?			
6. Is the material of good design?			
7. Does the piece of material actively involve the children?			
8. Is the material aesthetically pleasing?			
9. Does the value received by the children justify the time, effort, and expense (if any) involved?			

Caring for Materials

Durability is an important consideration when planning teacher made materials. Whenever possible, select heavy tagboard or construction paper. After constructing the material, cover it with clear Con-Tact paper, which can be purchased at most variety stores, or laminate it. The plastic coating strengthens the tagboard or paper and allows dirt, paint, or fingerprints to be wiped off. Most teachers prefer to laminate the material since it is usually a less expensive method of preservation. Lamination machines and film can be purchased through school supply stores. In fact, some school supply stores provide lamination as a service for a nominal fee.

Additional suggestions for caring and protecting materials include:

1. Use felt scraps, or damp tissue and paper towels, to remove crayon, grease pencil, and water-soluble ink from laminated materials.
2. Spray materials prepared from fabric with stain repellent.
3. Store materials of similar size in portfolio envelopes, which can be purchased at art supply stores.
4. Remove and repair damaged materials as soon as observed.

Storing Materials

For easy reference, store all materials for the writing center in the same box or location. Another suggestion is to store all materials related to one theme together. Likewise, it is helpful to store materials for similar skill levels together.

Properly storing materials will enhance their longevity. Small pieces of materials can be stored in envelopes, self-sealing transparent bags, manilla folders, or boxes. Large charts should be stored on a flat surface to avoid warping.

C H A P T E R 1

COLORS • COLORED MUFFINS • COLORED POPSICLES • COLORS OF APPLES • COLOR WORDS • CRAYONS • CUPCAKES • FALL LEAVES • PAINT BOX • POTTED FLOWERS • SOCKS • WHAT COLOR IS EACH FLOWER? • WHICH THINGS ARE RED? • TRAFFIC LIGHT

COLORS

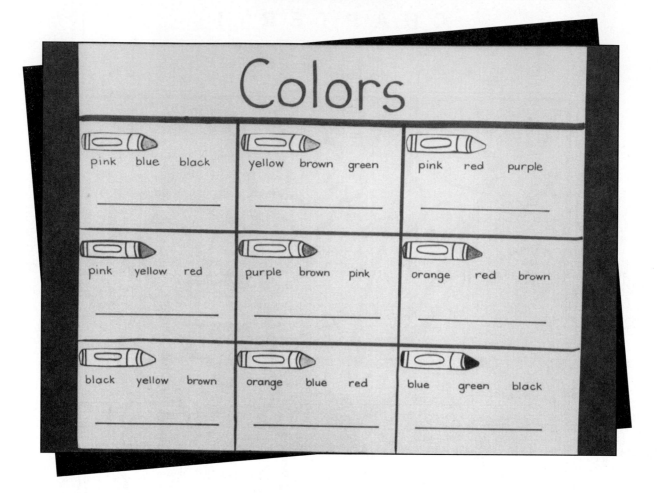

DEVELOPMENTAL GOALS:

1. To identify color words
2. To communicate in writing
3. To develop an appreciation for the printed word
4. To practice right-to-left progression skills
5. To practice using writing tools

RELATED CURRICULUM THEMES:

Art   Colors   We Create
Writing   Communication   Writing Tools

DIRECTIONS:

1. Select a sheet of tagboard paper in a color—such as light blue, light green, or white—that will complement basic crayon colors.

2. Print the title Colors across the top of the tagboard with a broad felt-tip marker. (*See photograph.*)

3. Using a lead pencil and ruler, divide the chart into nine boxes of equal size, as illustrated.

4. Trace over the pencil drawings with a medium felt-tip marker.

5. Cut nine sheets of paper, two-by-five inches each. Draw a crayon shape on each of the sheets. Color each crayon shape with a different marker, using blue, green, pink, red, purple, brown, yellow, orange, and black.

6. Under each crayon, print the names of three colors. One of the names should identify the color used in each case.

7. Draw a line three inches below the crayon names.

8. Cover the chart with clear Con-Tact paper or laminate it.

TOOLS AND ACCESSORIES:

- Watercolor markers
- Crayons
- Crayon wrappers, carefully removed
- Grease pencil
- Damp cloth/sponge

VARIATIONS AND EXTENSIONS:

1. The children could circle the correct answer (color name).

2. The children could print the color name on the line.

3. Prepare another chart without the names.

4. The children could prepare their own charts.

COLORED MUFFINS

red

green

yellow

orange

pink

DEVELOPMENTAL GOALS:

1. To identify the colors red, green, yellow, orange, and pink
2. To develop an appreciation of the printed word
3. To develop problem-solving skills
4. To recognize alphabet letters

RELATED CURRICULUM THEMES:

Foods

Our World

Colors

Breads

Celebrations

Cooking

DIRECTIONS:

1. Trace and cut from brown construction paper a muffin cup-shaped holder.
2. Cut muffin-top shapes from pieces of red, green, yellow, orange, and pink construction paper. Glue onto the muffin cups.
3. Trace the shape of the muffin cup vertically on the right side of the tagboard. (*See photograph.*)
4. Cut five pieces of manuscript paper. If unavailable, make the strip by two straight horizontal lines one inch apart. Measure 1/2 inch down by the top line and draw a broken line.
5. On each piece of manuscript paper, print the name of a different color: red, green, yellow, orange, and pink.
6. Cover the chart with clear Con-Tact paper or laminate it.

TOOLS AND ACCESSORIES:

- Watercolor markers
- Crayons
- Grease pencil
- Damp cloth/sponge

VARIATIONS AND EXTENSIONS:

1. If developmentally appropriate, add other colored muffins such as purple, brown, black, gold, and aqua.
2. Make the material self-correcting by printing the name of the color on the back of each muffin.

COLORED POPSICLES

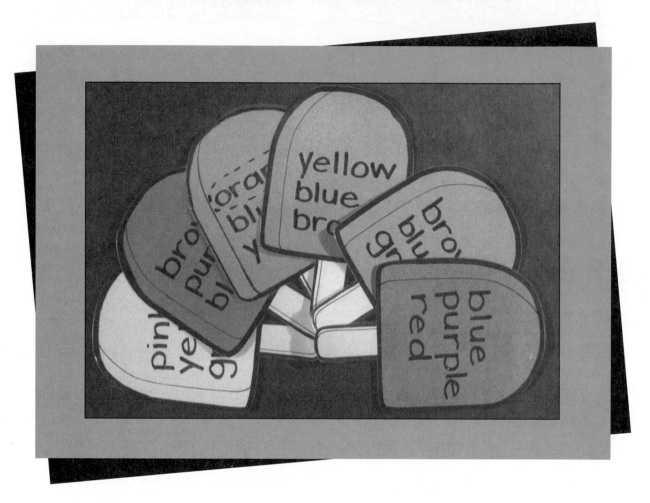

DEVELOPMENTAL GOALS:

1. To associate a color with the printed word
2. To develop an appreciation for the printed word
3. To develop visual discrimination skills
4. To develop problem-solving skills
5. To develop eye-hand coordination skills
6. To practice forming alphabet letters and numerals
7. To develop small-muscle coordination skills

RELATED CURRICULUM THEMES:

Colors

Summer Fun

Holidays

We Create

Foods

Words

DIRECTIONS:

1. Trace Popsicle shapes on pieces of yellow, brown, orange, blue, green, and purple construction paper. (*See photograph.*)
2. Cut six handles from beige construction paper.
3. Paste or glue a handle to each Popsicle.
4. Print the name of the color used and two additional color names on each Popsicle.
5. Add detail using a black felt-tip marker.
6. Cover with clear Con-Tact paper or laminate it.

TOOLS AND ACCESSORIES:

- Watercolor markers
- Crayons
- Grease pencil
- Damp cloth/sponge

VARIATIONS AND EXTENSIONS:

1. If developmentally appropriate, substitute other colors such as magenta, violet, and turquoise.
2. Omit writing the names of colors on each Popsicle. Let the children identify each color by recording its name.

COLORS OF APPLES

Colors of apples.

red red

green green

yellow yellow

DEVELOPMENTAL GOALS:

1. To identify the three colors of apples: red, green, and yellow
2. To practice forming alphabet letters
3. To associate the written word with a color
4. To communicate in writing
5. To develop an appreciation of the printed word

RELATED CURRICULUM THEMES:

Apples	Gardens	Colors
Seasons	Health	Shapes
Flowers	Fruits	Weather
Senses	Plants	Soil

DIRECTIONS:

1. Print the words Colors of apples across the top of a sheet of tagboard or heavy construction paper.
2. Cut apple shapes from pieces of red, green, and yellow construction paper.
3. Glue the apples on the sheet of paper.
4. Print the name of the color of the apple beside each piece of fruit twice. (*See photograph.*) Use regular letters once, and repeat using broken-line letters.
5. Cover the chart with clear Con-Tact paper or laminate it.

TOOLS AND ACCESSORIES:

- Watercolor markers
- Crayons
- Damp cloth/sponge
- Grease pencil

VARIATIONS AND EXTENSIONS:

1. Add another set of lines, and have the children print the color word independently.
2. Make another chart that doesn't identify the colors of the apples. Provide a line for the children to print the color names.

COLOR WORDS

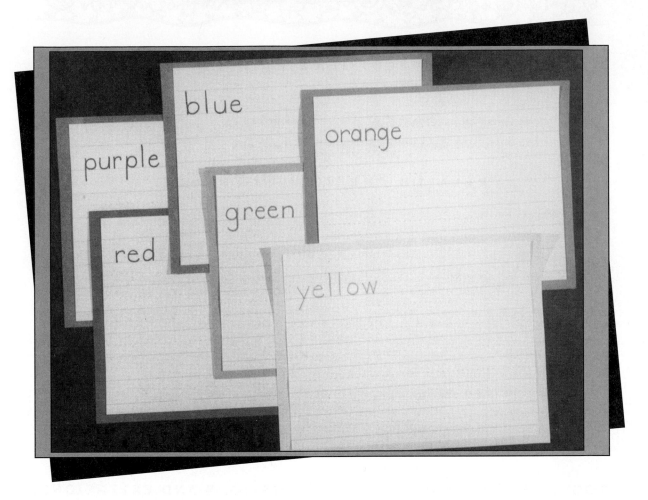

DEVELOPMENTAL GOALS:

1. To develop an appreciation for the printed word
2. To practice forming letters
3. To communicate in writing
4. To identify color words
5. To develop eye-hand coordination skills

RELATED CURRICULUM THEMES:

Colors
Symbols

Writing
Signs and Pictures

Words
All About Me

DIRECTIONS:

1. Glue pieces of manuscript paper on slightly larger pieces of colored construction paper. (*See photograph*.) Use green, orange, yellow, blue, red, black, purple, pink, and violet construction paper for the mats.
2. Print the names of the mat colors on the top lines of the manuscript papers.
3. Cover with clear Con-Tact paper or laminate it.

TOOLS AND ACCESSORIES:

- Watercolor markers
- Crayons
- Grease pencil
- Colored pencils
- Damp cloth/sponge

VARIATIONS AND EXTENSIONS:

1. If developmentally appropriate, expand the activity. For example, on the second line of the manuscript paper, print with broken lines A tree is green. Repeat for all of the other colors.
2. An object of the corresponding color could be added to each chart.

CRAYONS

DEVELOPMENTAL GOALS:

1. To develop an appreciation for the printed word
2. To communicate in writing
3. To practice correct forming of letters
4. To develop small-muscle coordination skills
5. To identify the printed names of colors

RELATED CURRICULUM THEMES:

Colors

We Create

Shapes

Writing Tools

Art

Writing Surfaces

DIRECTIONS:

1. Collect an assortment of colored tagboard: red, blue, green, purple, yellow, brown, orange, black, and pink.

2. Trace a crayon shape on each piece of colored tagboard. (*See photograph*.)

3. Use a matching felt-tip marker to make broken lines for the letters in the word for each color and draw the crayon tip and label. On the white tagboard, use a black marker.

4. Cover with clear Con-Tact paper or laminate it.

TOOLS AND ACCESSORIES:

- Watercolor markers
- Crayons
- Damp cloth/sponge

VARIATIONS AND EXTENSIONS:

1. Prepare crayons for the children to make.

2. Provide colored paper for the children to make their own crayons.

3. Use on a bulletin board, or prepare a color chart.

CUPCAKES

DEVELOPMENTAL GOALS:

1. To practice tracing letters of different colors
2. To discriminate between and among colors
3. To develop problem-solving skills (discrimination skills)
4. To practice correct letter formation
5. To communicate in writing
6. To develop small-muscle coordination skills

RELATED CURRICULUM THEMES:

Colors	Food	Writing Tools
Occupations	Health	We Create
Special Days	Senses	Safety
Family	Directions	Friends
Celebrations	Cooking	Breads

DIRECTIONS:

1. Cut sixteen pieces of tagboard or heavy construction paper into eight-by-eleven-inch pieces.
2. Draw a cupcake shape on each piece. (*See photograph.*)
3. Cut a piece of manuscript writing paper for each piece of tagboard. If manuscript paper is unavailable, draw lines. (*See photograph.*)
4. Glue the manuscript paper to the colored sheet of paper.
5. Color each of the cupcakes a different primary or secondary color.
6. On the top manuscript line, print the name of the color used for each cupcake.

TOOLS AND ACCESSORIES:

- Watercolor markers
- Crayons
- Damp cloth/sponge
- Grease pencils

VARIATIONS AND EXTENSIONS:

1. The children could prepare their own set of cupcakes.
2. Other objects, such as ice cream cones, cakes, shoes, balloons, jacks, balls, cars, or wagons, could be substituted for the cupcakes.

FALL LEAVES

DEVELOPMENTAL GOALS:

1. To associate a color with the printed word
2. To develop an appreciation for the printed word
3. To develop visual discrimination skills
4. To develop problem-solving skills
5. To develop eye-hand coordination skills
6. To practice forming alphabet letters
7. To develop small-muscle coordination skills

RELATED CURRICULUM THEMES:

Nature

Colors

Fall

Communication

Leaves

Our World

DIRECTIONS:

1. Across the top of a tagboard piece, print the title Fall leaves.
2. Draw a horizontal line 1/2 to 1 inch below the title. (*See photograph.*)
3. Divide the remainder of the chart into six sections.
4. Sketch a tree in the first section. Add color with felt-tip markers.
5. Draw a leaf in the remaining five boxes.
6. Color each leaf a different color: brown, red, green, yellow, and orange.
7. Add details using a felt-tip marker.
8. Print, using broken lines, the name of the color of each leaf under it.
9. Cover the chart with clear Con-Tact paper or laminate it.

TOOLS AND ACCESSORIES:

- Watercolor markers
- Crayons
- Grease pencil
- Damp cloth/sponge

VARIATIONS AND EXTENSIONS:

1. If developmentally appropriate, the color names could be omitted. This would allow children to write the color words without assistance.
2. Other objects could be used instead of leaves.

PAINT BOX

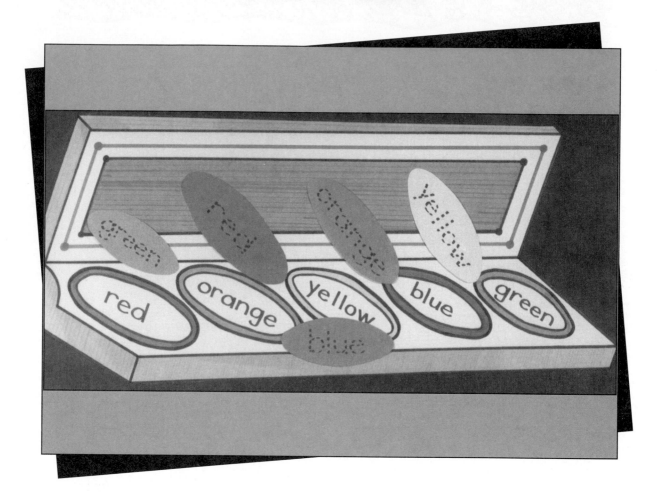

DEVELOPMENTAL GOALS:

1. To identify color words
2. To develop an appreciation for the printed word
3. To develop visual discrimination skills
4. To develop problem-solving skills
5. To develop eye-hand coordination skills
6. To practice forming alphabet letters and numerals
7. To develop small-muscle coordination skills

RELATED CURRICULUM THEMES:

Colors

Words

Our World

We Create

Art

Communication

DIRECTIONS:

1. Sketch a paint box on a piece of tagboard. (*See photograph.*)
2. Add oval shapes for each color.
3. Print the name of a different color in each oval: red, orange, yellow, blue, and green.
4. Circle each oval with the same color.
5. Add color to the box and details with oil pastels or a felt-tip marker.
6. Cover the chart with clear Con-Tact paper or laminate it.

TOOLS AND ACCESSORIES:

- Watercolor markers
- Crayons
- Grease pencil
- Damp cloth/sponge

VARIATIONS AND EXTENSIONS:

If developmentally appropriate, substitute other colors such as purple, brown, magenta, aqua, and turquoise.

POTTED FLOWERS

DEVELOPMENTAL GOALS:

1. To identify color words
2. To develop an awareness of the printed word
3. To develop eye–hand coordination skills
4. To practice forming alphabet letters
5. To communicate in writing
6. To develop small-muscle coordination skills

RELATED CURRICULUM THEMES:

Flowers

Plants

Colors

My World

Gardens

Flower Shop

DIRECTIONS:

1. Trace and cut flower-pot shapes out of brown construction paper.

2. Trace and cut an equal number of tulip shapes out of various colors of construction paper.

3. Trace and cut stems and leaves out of green construction paper.

4. Assemble the pieces to create potted flowers. (*See photograph.*)

5. On each flower pot, print three color words. One word must correspond with the color of the flower in that pot.

6. On each tulip, use a ruler and marker to draw a straight line.

7. Cover the finished pieces with clear Con-Tact paper or laminate them.

TOOLS AND ACCESSORIES:

- Watercolor markers
- Grease pencils
- Damp cloth/sponge

VARIATIONS AND EXTENSIONS:

1. Color choices could be omitted from the flower pots.

2. Objects could be substituted to reflect the curriculum theme.

SOCKS

DEVELOPMENTAL GOALS:

1. To practice forming letters
2. To communicate in writing
3. To develop an appreciation for the printed word

4. To develop eye–hand coordination
5. To develop small-muscle coordination skills
6. To associate a color with the printed word

RELATED CURRICULUM THEMES:

Colors	Clothes	Letters
The Alphabet	Shapes	Signs
Communication	Our World	Puzzles

DIRECTIONS:

1. Select colored construction paper or tagboard. Include the colors red, purple, orange, yellow, white, and green.
2. Trace the shape of a sock on each piece of tagboard.
3. Use a felt-tip marker to add detail. Trace around the shape of the entire sock, and add a toe line and stripes on the cuff. (See *photograph*.)
4. Use broken lines to print the color word on each sock.
5. Cut each sock into two pieces, varying the shape of the cut.
6. Cover the finished pieces with clear Con-Tact paper or laminate them.

TOOLS AND ACCESSORIES:

- Watercolor markers
- Crayons
- Grease pencil
- Damp cloth/sponge

VARIATIONS AND EXTENSIONS:

1. Have the children trace the lines on each sock.
2. On the reverse side, have the children print the color name of the sock freehand.
3. The children could match the tops of the socks and trace the letters.
4. The children could prepare a set of socks.

WHAT COLOR IS EACH FLOWER?

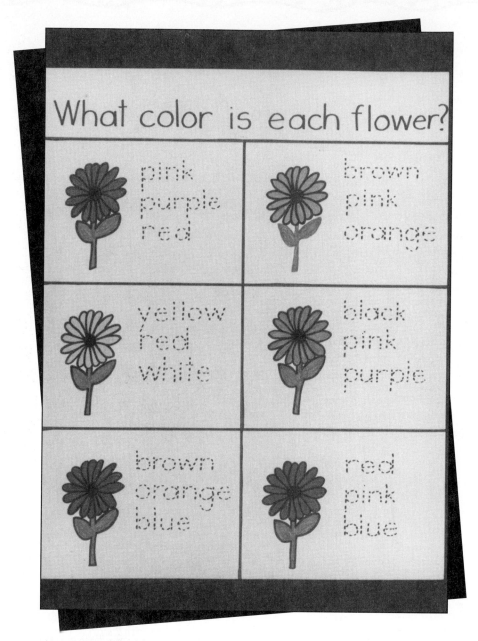

What color is each flower?

pink purple red	brown pink orange
yellow red white	black pink purple
brown orange blue	red pink blue

DEVELOPMENTAL GOALS:

1. To identify color words
2. To develop eye–hand coordination skills
3. To practice the forming of alphabet letters
4. To communicate through writing

RELATED CURRICULUM THEMES:

Flowers

Words

Alphabet Letters

Science

Art

Colors

DIRECTIONS:

1. Print the title What color is each flower? across the top of a large sheet of tagboard.
2. Draw a horizontal line under the title.
3. Divide the remainder of the tagboard sheet into six equal sections.
4. Draw a flower in each section.
5. Color each flower using a different color marker or CRAY-PAS.
6. In each box, print, using broken lines, the name of the color used and two others.
7. Cover chart with clear Con-Tact paper or laminate it.

TOOLS AND ACCESSORIES:

- Watercolor markers
- Crayons
- Grease pencils
- Damp cloth/sponge

VARIATIONS AND EXTENSIONS:

1. The children could draw a line from the flower to the name of the correct color.
2. If developmentally appropriate, the chart could be made with a line for the children to print the name of the correct color.
3. A chart could be made using other objects related to a theme.

WHICH THINGS ARE RED?

Which things are red?

(snowman)	yes	no
(firefighter helmet 12)	yes	no
(school bus)	yes	no
(STOP sign)	yes	no
(heart)	yes	no

DEVELOPMENTAL GOALS:

1. To practice forming letters
2. To develop eye–hand coordination skills
3. To communicate in writing
4. To develop visual discrimination skills
5. To develop problem-solving skills

RELATED CURRICULUM THEMES:

Colors	Seasons	Transportation
Safety	Clothes/Hats	Signs
Weather	Community Helpers	Fire Fighters
Shapes	Clothes	Writing
Winter	Valentine's Day	Wheels

DIRECTIONS:

1. Print the title Which things are red? across the top of a large piece of tagboard, using a felt-tip marker. Use a black marker for the first three words. The word Red should be printed with a red marker.
2. Draw the corresponding illustrations. Color if desired. (*See photograph.*)
3. Print the words Yes and No, using broken lines.
4. Cover the chart with clear Con-Tact paper or laminate it.

TOOLS AND ACCESSORIES:

- Watercolor markers—black, red, yellow, pink
- Crayons
- Damp cloth/sponge

VARIATIONS AND EXTENSIONS:

1. The children could trace the correct response.
2. The children could design their own charts.

TRAFFIC LIGHTS

DEVELOPMENTAL GOALS:

1. To identify the colors red, green, and yellow
2. To communicate in writing
3. To practice forming letters
4. To develop eye–hand coordination skills
5. To identify the three colors of traffic lights

RELATED CURRICULUM THEMES:

Communication

Travel

Colors

Occupations

Safety

Signs

Our Town

Shapes

Transportation

DIRECTIONS:

1. Print across the top of a piece of tagboard the title Traffic Lights. (*See photograph.*)

2. Cut three silhouettes of traffic lights from black construction paper and paste onto the tagboard. (*See photograph.*)

3. Cut one bold colored red, yellow, and green circle. Then cut two lighter shades for each of the three colors.

4. Paste the bright red circle at the top of the first traffic light. Below this, paste the lighter-colored yellow circle. Under the yellow circle, paste the light-green circle.

5. Paste a light red on the top of the second traffic light, followed by a bold yellow circle and lighter-green circle.

6. On the third traffic light, paste a light-red circle at the top. Under this, paste a lighter-yellow circle. The green circle can be pasted at the bottom.

7. Print, using a broken line, the word red under the first traffic light, yellow under the second traffic light, and green under the third traffic light.

8. Cover the chart with clear Con-Tact paper or laminate it.

TOOLS AND ACCESSORIES:

- Watercolor markers red, green, yellow (black)
- Crayons, red, yellow, green (black)
- Damp cloth/sponge

VARIATIONS AND EXTENSIONS:

1. Extend this experience by adding another chart—
   - A red light means stop.
   - A green light means go.
   - A yellow light means caution.

2. Provide supplies for the children to construct their own traffic light pictures.

CHAPTER 2

BALLOONS • BROWN BEARS • EGGS • FIRE HAT NUMBER SEQUENCING • HOW MANY DOTS ARE IN EACH SET? • NUMBER CARDS • NUMERALS • NUMERALS–CLOTHING • 1–ONE • OUR NUMBERS • SETS OF OBJECTS • SNOWMEN • STICKER COUNTING 1–6 • TELEPHONE NUMBERS • TULIPS

Balloons

five 5

four 4

three 3

two 2

one 1

one 1

DEVELOPMENTAL GOALS:

1. To practice forming numerals
2. To associate numerals with the printed word
3. To develop eye–hand coordination skills
4. To develop visual discrimination skills

RELATED CURRICULUM THEMES:

Writing

Letters

Communication

Sets

Numbers

Air

DIRECTIONS:

1. Cut nine-by-twelve-inch pieces from a sheet of tagboard.
2. Across the top of the tagboard, draw manuscript lines. (*See photograph.*)
3. Draw two sets of lines across the bottom of the tagboard.
4. Print a number word, followed by its numeral, on the manuscript line at the top of each piece of paper.
5. Cut corresponding sets of balloon shapes from construction paper.
6. Glue the balloons onto the paper. Use a felt-tip marker to draw strings.
7. Print, using a broken line, the name and number on the manuscript line under the balloon.
8. Cover the finished pieces with clear Con-Tact paper or laminate them.

TOOLS AND ACCESSORIES:

- Watercolor markers
- Crayons
- Grease pencil
- Damp cloth/sponge

VARIATIONS AND EXTENSIONS:

1. Vary objects to represent the children's interests or a curriculum theme.
2. Depending on the developmental level of the children, vary the numerals to challenge them.

BROWN BEARS

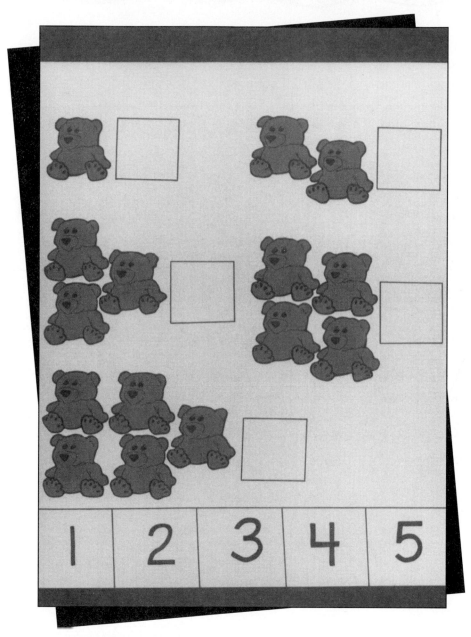

DEVELOPMENTAL GOALS:

1. To identify sets of objects
2. To match numerals to the number of objects in a set
3. To develop visual discrimination skills
4. To develop problem-solving skills
5. To develop eye–hand coordination skills
6. To practice forming numerals
7. To develop small-muscle coordination skills

RELATED CURRICULUM THEMES:

Bears

Toys

Numerals

Animals

Zoo Animals

Writing

DIRECTIONS:

1. Using a ruler as a guide, draw a horizontal line four inches from the bottom of a sheet of tagboard.
2. Draw vertical lines every four inches to create five four-inch squares.
3. Trace fifteen bears on a piece of brown tagboard. (*See photograph.*)
4. Cut out the bears.
5. Outline the bears and add details such as eyes, nose, and mouth with a black felt-tip marker.
6. Glue the bears to the chart as illustrated.
7. Draw a box next to set of bears.
8. Cover chart with clear Con-Tact paper or laminate it.

TOOLS AND ACCESSORIES:

- Watercolor markers
- Crayons
- Grease pencil
- Damp cloth/sponge

VARIATIONS AND EXTENSIONS:

1. The bears could be replaced with objects related to another theme.
2. If developmentally appropriate, the number of objects could be increased.
3. Children could be encouraged to write the number word in the boxes.

Eggs

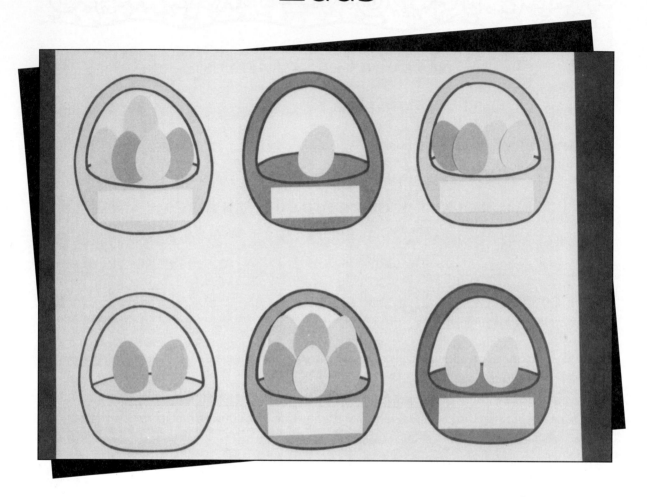

DEVELOPMENTAL GOALS:

1. To identify the number of objects in set

2. To practice forming numerals and alphabet letters

3. To develop eye–hand coordination skills

4. To develop an appreciation for the printed word

RELATED CURRICULUM THEMES:

Numbers   Foods   Words

Containers   Easter   Eggs

DIRECTIONS:

1. Trace and cut six baskets from different colors of construction paper. (*See photograph*.)

2. Glue the baskets onto a large piece of tagboard.

3. Cut a strip of manuscript paper to fit on each basket. If unavailable, make the strip by drawing two horizontal lines one inch apart. Draw a row of broken lines.

4. Cut eggs out of construction paper. Glue a different number of eggs in each basket.

5. Cover the chart with clear Con-Tact paper or laminate it.

TOOLS AND ACCESSORIES:

- Watercolor markers
- Crayons
- Construction paper

VARIATIONS AND EXTENSIONS:

1. Depending on the developmental level of the children, increase or decrease the number of eggs in each basket.

2. Prepare six word cards, each with the name of the numbers used.

FIRE HAT NUMBER SEQUENCING

DEVELOPMENTAL GOALS:

1. Match a numeral with the appropriate printed word
2. To practice forming letters
3. To communicate in writing
4. To practice fine motor skills
5. To develop eye–hand coordination skills
6. To develop visual discrimination skills

RELATED CURRICULUM THEMES:

Colors   Occupations   Safety

Hats   Clothing   Tools

DIRECTIONS:

1. Cut eight-by-eight-inch squares from white tagboard.

2. Using a picture of a fire fighter's hat as a model, trace it onto each of the pieces of tagboard. (*See photograph.*)

3. Add color to each of the hats by using a red felt-tip marker or CRAY-PAS piece. A black marker can be used to add detail and to draw the underside of the hat.

4. Print, using a broken line, a different numeral on each hat.

5. Cover the finished pieces with clear Con-Tact paper or laminate them.

TOOLS AND ACCESSORIES:

- Watercolor markers
- Crayons
- Grease pencil
- Damp cloth/sponge

VARIATIONS AND EXTENSIONS:

1. This activity can be adapted to almost any theme.

2. If developmentally appropriate, extend beyond the number six.

3. Use permanent felt-tip markers to print the numeral on the contact paper or laminate it. The markings can be removed using hair spray and adapted to the individual needs of children.

HOW MANY DOTS ARE IN EACH SET?

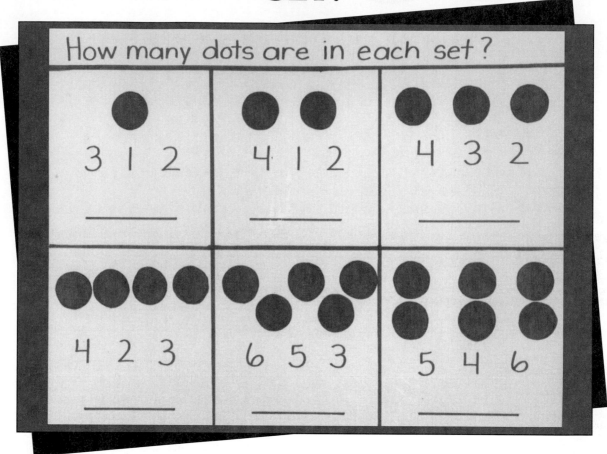

How many dots are in each set?

3 1 2	4 1 2	4 3 2
___	___	___
4 2 3	6 5 3	5 4 6
___	___	___

DEVELOPMENTAL GOALS:

1. To recognize the relationship between numerals and symbols

2. To become familiar with printed numerals

3. To practice numeral formation

4. To develop small-muscle coordination skills

5. To develop eye–hand coordination skills

6. To develop an understanding of the concept of a set

RELATED CURRICULUM THEMES:

Communication   Numerals   Shapes

Sets   Counting   Writing

DIRECTIONS:

1. Print the title How many dots are there in each set? across the top of a sheet of tagboard.

2. Using a ruler and soft-lead pencil, lightly divide the remainder of space into six squares.

3. Draw one dot in the first square, two in the second square, three in the third square, four in the fourth square, five in the fifth square, and six in the last square.

4. Under each set of dots, record three numerals. In each case, one of the numerals needs to correspond to the number of dots in that set.

5. Three or four inches under the numerals, provide a line for the children to write a response.

6. Cover the chart with clear Con-Tact paper or laminate it.

TOOLS AND ACCESSORIES:

- Watercolor markers
- Crayons
- Grease pencil
- Damp cloth/sponge

VARIATIONS AND EXTENSIONS:

1. The children could circle the numeral that corresponds to the number of dots in each square.

2. The chart could be prepared with other symbols.

3. If a child has mastered all of the above, tell him/her to print the numeral that comes before the one that has been circled and the numeral that comes after it.

NUMBER CARDS

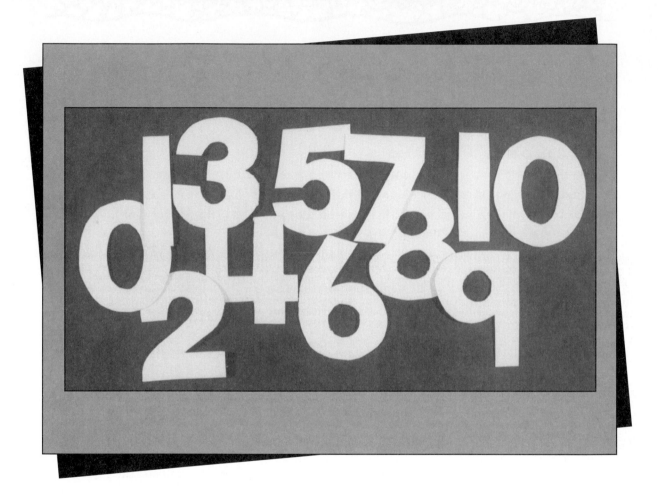

DEVELOPMENTAL GOALS:

1. To practice forming the numerals 1–9
2. To communicate in writing
3. To develop eye–hand coordination skills
4. To develop small-muscle coordination skills

RELATED CURRICULUM THEMES:

Numbers	Writing Tools	Writing Surfaces
Things in My World	Communication	Shapes

DIRECTIONS:

1. Cut out the numerals in the appendix.
2. Trace the numeral patterns onto heavy tagboard.
3. Cut out the numerals using a scissors or craft knife.
4. Cover the cards with clear Con-Tact paper or laminate.

TOOLS AND ACCESSORIES:

- Watercolor markers
- Crayons
- Grease pencil
- Chalk
- Colored pencils
- Pens
- Paper
- Cardboard
- Styrofoam
- Chalkboard
- Aluminum foil
- Foil
- Paint and paintbrushes

VARIATIONS AND EXTENSIONS:

1. The children could prepare number books.
2. Show the children how to do crayon rubbings. Place a sheet of paper over a numeral stencil. Color over the stencil with the flat side of a crayon.

Numerals

DEVELOPMENTAL GOALS:

1. To associate numerals with the printed word
2. To develop an appreciation for the printed word
3. To develop visual discrimination skills
4. To develop problem-solving skills
5. To develop eye–hand coordination skills
6. To develop small-muscle coordination skills

RELATED CURRICULUM THEMES:

Writing	Sets	Toys
Numbers	Alphabet	My World

DIRECTIONS:

1. Print across a piece of tagboard the title Numerals.
2. Draw a horizontal line under the title.
3. Divide the remainder of the tagboard into six boxes.
4. Draw objects in each box.
5. Color the objects with felt-tip markers to add interest.
6. Record the numeral that identifies the set in the lower left corner of each box.
7. Print three different names of numbers in the lower right side of each box. One of the numbers should represent the number of objects in the set.
8. Cover the chart with clear Con-Tact paper or laminate it.

TOOLS AND ACCESSORIES:

- Watercolor markers
- Crayons
- Grease pencil
- Damp cloth/sponge

VARIATIONS AND EXTENSIONS:

1. Create a reference chart that shows numbers expressed as both words and numerals.
2. If developmentally appropriate, increase the number of objects in each set.
3. Substitute objects that relate to a curriculum theme.

NUMERALS–CLOTHING

Numerals

3 _____

2 _____

2 _____

0 _____

1 _____

1 _____

DEVELOPMENTAL GOALS:

1. To identify sets of objects
2. To identify numerals
3. To develop visual discrimination skills
4. To develop problem-solving skills
5. To develop eye–hand coordination skills
6. To practice forming alphabet letters
7. To develop small-muscle coordination skills

RELATED CURRICULUM THEMES:

Clothing	My World	Communication
Writing	Numbers	Sets

DIRECTIONS:

1. Divide a piece of tagboard into six sections of equal size. (*See photograph.*)
2. Sketch, or cut and paste, a picture of a piece or pieces of clothing or accessories in each box.
3. Add color and details with CRAY-PAS and/or felt-tip markers.
4. Print the corresponding numeral beneath each picture.
5. Draw a line under each object.
6. Cover the chart with clear Con-Tact paper or laminate it.

TOOLS AND ACCESSORIES:

- Watercolor markers
- Crayons
- Grease pencil
- Damp cloth/sponge

VARIATIONS AND EXTENSIONS:

1. The objects pictured could reflect the curriculum theme.
2. If developmentally appropriate, other items could be substituted such as suspenders, gown, visor, thongs, and sandals.

1–ONE

DEVELOPMENTAL GOALS:

1. To associate a numeral with the printed word
2. To develop an appreciation for the printed word
3. To develop eye–hand coordination skills
4. To practice forming letters
5. To communicate in writing
6. To develop small-muscle coordination skills
7. To develop visual discrimination skills

RELATED CURRICULUM THEMES:

Numbers   Sets   Communication

Symbols   Signs   Words

DIRECTIONS:

1. Print a numeral on the top line of a piece of manuscript paper. (*See photograph.*)
2. On the third line of the paper, print the numeral using a broken line.
3. Print the word for the numeral on the fifth line.
4. Print the word, using a broken line, on the seventh line.
5. Cover the finished piece with clear Con-Tact paper or laminate it.

TOOLS AND ACCESSORIES:

- Watercolor markers
- Crayons
- Grease pencil
- Damp cloth/sponge

VARIATIONS AND EXTENSIONS:

1. As the children progress in numeral identification, prepare cards with numerals with increasing value.
2. Prepare charts leaving enough space so that the children can draw objects to represent the numerals.

OUR NUMBERS

Our numbers	
Draw four bees.	Draw two trees.
Draw six bats.	Draw five cats.
Draw one hat.	Draw three mats.

DEVELOPMENTAL GOALS:

1. To develop an appreciation for the printed word
2. To develop eye–hand coordination skills
3. To develop small-muscle coordination skills
4. To follow written directions

RELATED CURRICULUM THEMES:

Writing

Reading

Numbers

Our World

Word Families

Writing Tools

DIRECTIONS:

1. Write the title Our numbers on a sheet of tagboard.
2. Use a ruler and marker to divide the sheet into six boxes.
3. In each box, write a direction. (*See photograph.*)
4. Cover the chart with clear Con-Tact paper or laminate it.

TOOLS AND ACCESSORIES:

- Watercolor markers
- Crayons
- Damp cloth/sponge
- Assortment of corresponding laminated pictures

VARIATIONS AND EXTENSIONS:

1. Change the items to correspond with the curriculum theme.
2. Change the number of items requested to make the material developmentally appropriate.
3. Prepare individual picture pieces and place them in a container next to the chart. The children can then select the cards and place them in the appropriate box.
4. Draw a square to be added in the upper left corner of each box, providing the children a place to write the correct numeral.

SETS OF OBJECTS

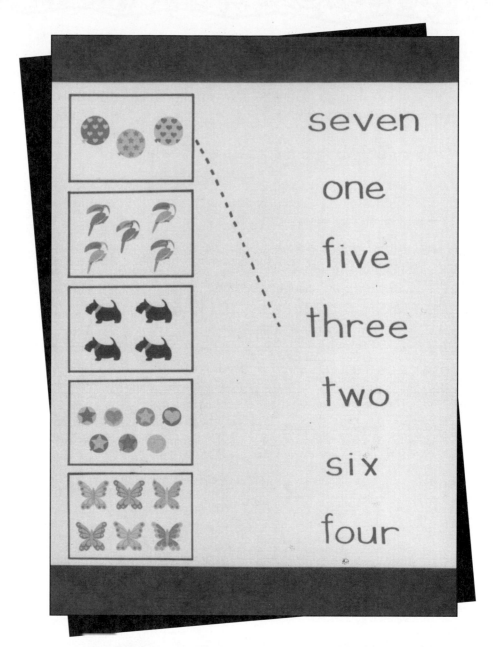

seven

one

five

three

two

six

four

DEVELOPMENTAL GOALS:

1. To associate the printed number word with a set of objects
2. To develop an appreciation for the printed word
3. To develop visual discrimination skills
4. To develop problem-solving skills
5. To develop eye–hand coordination skills
6. To develop small-muscle coordination skills

RELATED CURRICULUM THEMES:

Words	Sets	Numbers
Communication	Our World	Symbols

DIRECTIONS:

1. Draw five boxes down the left side of a piece of tagboard. (*See photograph.*)
2. Draw objects, or place stickers of objects, in each box.
3. On seven strips of manuscript paper, print the words for the numbers one through seven.
4. Paste or glue the numeral words down the right side of the tagboard.
5. Draw broken lines from the first box to the corresponding number word.
6. Cover the chart with clear Con-Tact paper or laminate it.

TOOLS AND ACCESSORIES:

- Watercolor markers
- Crayons
- Grease pencil
- Damp cloth/sponge

VARIATIONS AND EXTENSIONS:

1. If developmentally appropriate, increase the number of objects in each set.
2. Substitute numerals for the number words.

SNOWMEN

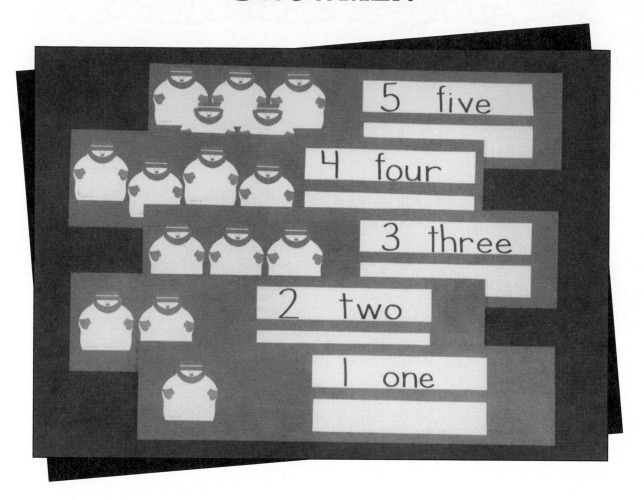

DEVELOPMENTAL GOALS:

1. To identify the numerals 1–5
2. To identify the printed words for the numerals 1–5
3. To practice forming numbers
4. To develop eye–hand coordination skills
5. To communicate through writing

RELATED CURRICULUM THEMES:

Numbers

Words

Communication

Seasons

Weather

Winter

DIRECTIONS:

1. Cut five-inch-wide horizontal strips from a piece of tagboard.

2. Cut snowmen figures from notepads, giftwrap, stickers, coloring books or draw pictures for each strip.

3. On the first strip, paste one figure. Paste two figures on the second strip, three on the third, four on the fourth, and five on the fifth.

4. Cut ten double-lined strips of manuscript writing seven inches in length.

5. Cover with clear Con-Tact paper or laminate.

TOOLS AND ACCESSORIES:

- Watercolor markers
- Crayons
- Damp cloth/sponge

VARIATIONS AND EXTENSIONS:

1. Change the symbols to correspond with a classroom theme or other holidays or seasons.

2. If developmentally appropriate, extend the number of sets.

STICKER COUNTING 1–6

DEVELOPMENTAL GOALS:

1. To develop an awareness of sets
2. To communicate in writing
3. To develop an appreciation for the printed word
4. To develop small-muscle coordination skills
5. To relate sets to the printed word
6. To practice correct letter formation

RELATED CURRICULUM THEMES:

Circus | Animals | Numbers
Fruits/Vegetables | Hats | Homes
Cars/Trucks/Buses | Clothing | Tools
Families | Numbers | Occupations
Pets | Plants | Shapes
Holidays | Wheels | Colors
Fantasy/Reality | Watches/Clocks | Friends
Money | Bugs | Machines
Nature | Sets | Collections

DIRECTIONS:

1. Cut tagboard into two eighteen-inch squares.
2. Divide each piece of tagboard into six six-inch squares using a soft-lead pencil.
3. Trace over the penciled lines on one piece of tagboard using a felt-tip marker.
4. Cut the second piece of tagboard into the six pieces, as outlined.
5. On a sheet of tagboard, glue sets of pictures or attach stickers. (*See photograph.*)
6. Under each set of stickers, print the corresponding number word.
7. On each of the six-inch squares, glue corresponding sets of items, using broken letters to print the corresponding number word.
8. Cover the cards with clear Con-Tact paper or laminate them.

TOOLS AND ACCESSORIES:

- Watercolor markers
- Crayons
- Damp cloth/sponge

VARIATIONS AND EXTENSIONS:

1. Provide materials for the children to construct their own cards.
2. Make a second board that provides space only to print the correct number.

TELEPHONE NUMBERS

DEVELOPMENTAL GOALS:

1. To learn home telephone numbers
2. To develop an appreciation for the printed word
3. To communicate in writing
4. To practice forming letters and numerals
5. To develop small-muscle coordination skills
6. To develop eye–hand coordination skills

RELATED CURRICULUM THEMES:

Communication   Friends   All About Me

Safety   Homes   Community Helpers

DIRECTIONS:

1. Draw or trace a telephone onto a piece of tagboard.

2. Use CRAY-PAS, crayons, or felt-tip markers to add color and detail. (*See photograph.*)

3. Print the numerals on the telephone.

4. Cover the finished piece with clear Con-Tact paper or laminate it.

5. Print each child's name and telephone number on an individual index card.

TOOLS AND ACCESSORIES:

- Watercolor markers
- Crayons
- Grease pencil
- Damp cloth/sponge
- On unlined index cards print the children's names and telephone numbers. Laminate to prepare for the children's use.

VARIATIONS AND EXTENSIONS:

1. The children can copy their friends' names and telephone numbers.

2. Prepare a chart of emergency telephone numbers that includes those for the fire department, police, and hospital.

3. Create a classroom bulletin board using a telephone chart and the children's telephone numbers.

TULIPS

DEVELOPMENTAL GOALS:

1. To match the written word with the symbols and sets

2. To recognize the numerals and sets 1–7

3. To develop an appreciation for the printed word

4. To develop eye–hand coordination skills

RELATED CURRICULUM THEMES:

Numbers	Colors	Words
Flowers	Weather	Gardens
Plants	Science	Bulbs

DIRECTIONS:

1. Cut a thirty-inch strip of tagboard.
2. Cut fourteen tulip shapes and seven stems from colored construction paper. (*See photograph.*)
3. Write a numeral on each of seven tulips, beginning with 1 for the first tulip. Continue, writing the numerals 2–7. (*See photograph.*)
4. Paste the seven tulips and stems on the tagboard.
5. Draw dots on the stem of each tulip to correspond with the numeral.
6. Write the name of the numeral for each of the remaining tulips. Begin with one. Continue with two, three, four, five, six, and seven.
7. Cover the finished piece with clear Con-Tact paper or laminate it.

TOOLS AND ACCESSORIES:

- Watercolor markers
- Crayons
- Colored construction paper

VARIATIONS AND EXTENSIONS:

1. Change the objects to correspond with a classroom theme.
2. If developmentally appropriate, use additional numerals.

CHAPTER 3

DEAR JOE,
HOW ARE
YOU? I AM
FINE.
SUE

LETTERS.

ALPHABET WATERMELON

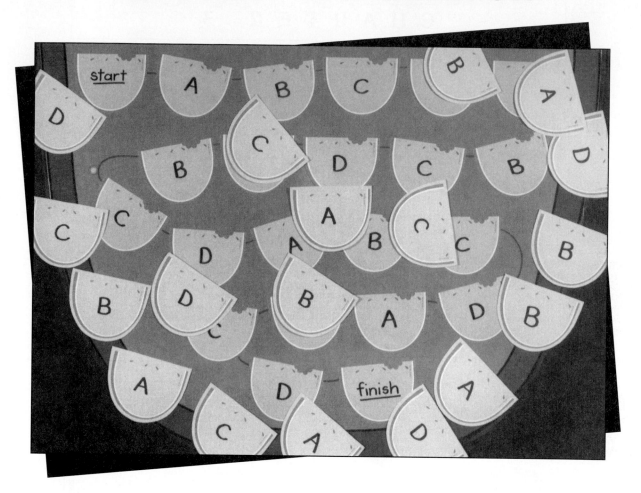

DEVELOPMENTAL GOALS:

1. To recognize uppercase alphabet letters
2. To practice problem-solving skills
3. To develop eye–hand coordination skills
4. To develop visual discrimination skills

RELATED CURRICULUM THEMES:

Letters
Nutrition
Seeds

Communication
Foods
Summer

Fruit
Writing
Colors

DIRECTIONS:

1. Draw a half of a watermelon on a pink piece of tagboard. (*See photograph.*)

2. Cut out the watermelon.

3. Draw the rind, and color the area green using CRAY-PAS or a felt-tip marker. Outline the edges of the rind with a black marker.

4. Construct two sets of small watermelon slices from colored construction paper. Add detail by outlining with a green marker or crayon.

5. Print the word START on one watermelon slice and FINISH on another. On the remaining letters, print uppercase alphabet letters. Repeat on the second set of watermelon slices.

6. Glue or paste the first set of letters on the watermelon. Use a green marker to draw a line from one melon to another, creating a game board pattern.

7. Cover the board and the pieces with clear Con-Tact paper or laminate them.

TOOLS AND ACCESSORIES:

- Watercolor markers
- Crayons
- Grease pencil
- Damp cloth/sponge

VARIATIONS AND EXTENSIONS:

1. Use lowercase letters or numerals.

2. The background shape could be another food, such as a squash, cantaloupe, or strawberry. This activity also could be adapted for holidays. Examples include a pumpkin for Halloween, a turkey for Thanksgiving, rabbits or eggs for Easter, and hearts for Valentine's Day.

CAPITAL LETTERS

Capital Letters
Write the correct word to begin each sentence.

1. (May-may)_____ John go?
2. (the-The)_____ ball is red.
3. (A-a)_____ dog barks.
4. (my-My)_____ shoes are blue.
5. (hens-Hens)_____ lay eggs.
6. (I-i) _____ can run.
7. (she-She) _____ likes apples.
8. (Did-did) _____ Maria fall?

DEVELOPMENTAL GOALS:

1. To practice writing capital letters
2. To develop an appreciation for the printed word
3. To develop visual discrimination skills
4. To develop problem-solving skills
5. To develop eye–hand coordination skills
6. To develop small-muscle coordination skills

RELATED CURRICULUM THEMES:

Symbols

Writing Tools

Communication

Our Alphabet

Writing

Reading

DIRECTIONS:

1. Print the title CAPITAL LETTERS across the top of a large piece of manuscript paper. (*See photograph.*)
2. Under the title, print the correct word to begin each sentence.
3. Leave a blank line. Then print the following:
   a. (May or may) _____ John go?
   b. (the or The) _____ ball is red.
   c. (A or a) _____ dog barks.
   d. (my or My) _____ shoes are blue.
   e. (hens or Hens) _____ lay eggs.
   f. (I or i) _____ can run.
   g. (she or She) _____ likes apples.
   h. (Did or did) _____ Maria fall?
4. Cover the finished piece with clear Con-Tact paper or laminate it.

TOOLS AND ACCESSORIES:

- Watercolor markers
- Crayons
- Grease pencil
- Damp cloth/sponge

VARIATIONS AND EXTENSIONS:

1. Make a chart that includes pronouns, such as we, me, mine, you, he, him, she, her, and yours.
2. Include culturally diverse names on the chart.

CIRCLE THE MATCHING LOWERCASE LETTER

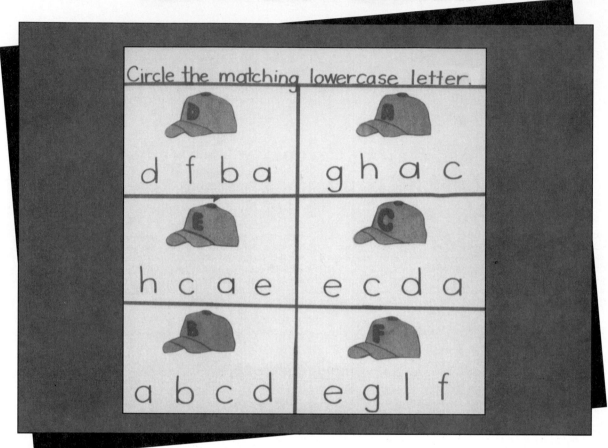

Circle the matching lowercase letter.

DEVELOPMENTAL GOALS:

1. To develop eye–hand coordination skills
2. To develop visual discrimination skills
3. To develop problem-solving skills
4. To identify and match uppercase and lowercase letters
5. To develop small muscle coordination skills

RELATED CURRICULUM THEMES:

Sports

Letters

Weather

Clothing

Hats

Occupations

DIRECTIONS:

1. Print the title Circle the matching lowercase letter across the top of a sheet of tagboard.
2. Use a ruler and soft-lead pencil to lightly divide the remainder of the chart into six squares.
3. Use a black felt-tip marker to trace over the pencil marks.
4. Draw and cut out six caps on a square of colored paper.
5. Print a different uppercase alphabet letter on each cap with a felt-tip marker.
6. If necessary, use a felt-tip marker to define the cap.
7. Glue a cap in each square.
8. Under each cap, print four lowercase letters, one of which corresponds to the letter on the cap.
9. Cover the chart with clear Con-Tact paper or laminate it.

TOOLS AND ACCESSORIES:

- Watercolor markers
- Crayons
- Damp cloth/sponge

VARIATIONS AND EXTENSIONS:

1. Use lowercase letters on the hats.
2. Use other objects on the chart.

CLOTHES ALPHABET

DEVELOPMENTAL GOALS:

1. To develop an appreciation for the printed word
2. To develop visual discrimination skills
3. To develop problem-solving skills
4. To develop eye–hand coordination skills
5. To practice forming alphabet letters
6. To develop small-muscle coordination skills

RELATED CURRICULUM THEMES:

Alphabet   Clothes   Writing
Communication   Symbols   Seasons

DIRECTIONS:

1. Cut a series of 8-inch x 9-inch cards from tagboard.
2. Print CLOTHES ALPHABET on the top card, using a felt-tip marker. (*See photograph.*)
3. Draw a different piece of clothing on each of the other cards. Suggested are:

   - tie   - apron   - shirt   - pants   - hat   - socks
   - skirt   - mitten   - scarf   - jacket   - shoes   - shorts

4. Add color to each drawing using felt-tip markers.
5. Use a black felt-tip marker to add details to each piece of clothing, if desired.
6. Across the top of each card draw a short line for each letter in the name of the article of clothing pictured.
7. Print the beginning alphabet letter for the article of clothing.
8. Cover the cards with clear Con-Tact paper or laminate them.

TOOLS AND ACCESSORIES:

- Watercolor markers
- Crayons
- Grease pencil
- Damp cloth/sponge

VARIATIONS AND EXTENSIONS:

1. Make the cards self-correcting by printing the word on the reverse side.
2. Adapt the concept to the curriculum theme.

DOCTORS' TOOLS

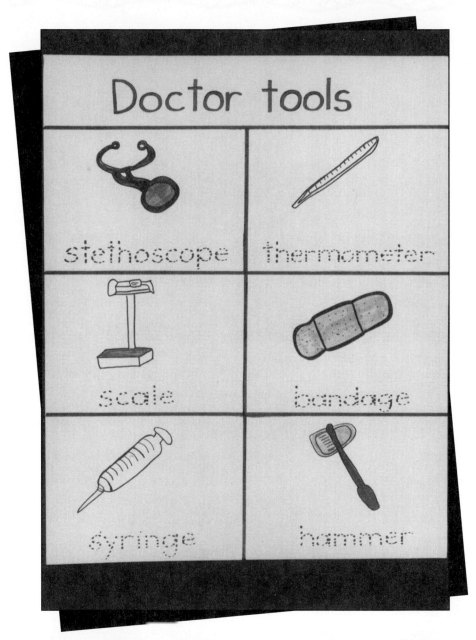

DEVELOPMENTAL GOALS:

1. To practice forming alphabet letters
2. To communicate in writing
3. To develop an appreciation for the printed word
4. To develop eye–hand coordination skills
5. To identify a doctor's tools

RELATED CURRICULUM THEMES:

Doctors/Nurses   Families   Health

Occupations   Tools   Community Helpers

People in My World   How I Care for Myself   Hospitals

DIRECTIONS:

1. Print the title Doctors' Tools across the top of a piece of tagboard. (*See photograph.*)
2. Divide the remainder of the tagboard into six sections of equal size, using a soft-lead pencil.
3. Trace over the lines with a felt-tip marker.
4. In each section, draw a different doctor's tool. Suggested are:
   - stethoscope
   - scale
   - syringe
   - thermometer
   - bandage
   - hammer
5. To add interest, color the objects with markers.
6. Print the name of each tool, using a broken line, under each picture.
7. Cover the chart with clear Con-Tact paper or laminate it.

TOOLS AND ACCESSORIES:

- Watercolor markers
- Grease pencil
- Damp cloth/sponge

VARIATIONS AND EXTENSIONS:

1. Extend the lesson by making charts for other occupations, such as baker, barber, mechanic, carpenter, fire fighter, and dentist.
2. To make the chart more challenging, prepare an identical one, but leave out the names of the objects and instead, draw a line on which the children can identify them.

DO THE OBJECTS BEGIN WITH A B OR AN S?

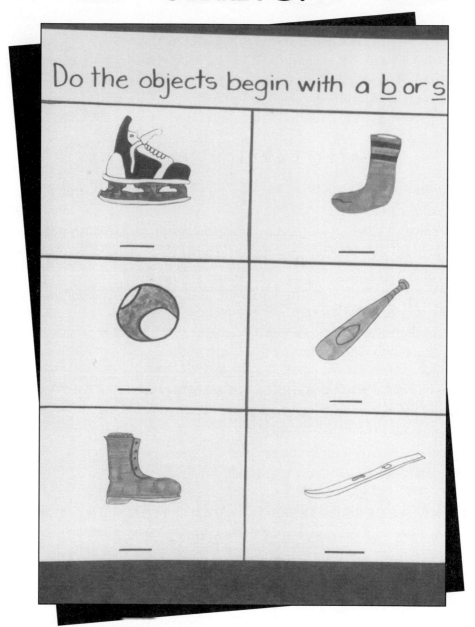

Do the objects begin with a b or s

DEVELOPMENTAL GOALS:

1. To distinguish between the *b* and *s* sounds
2. To practice forming the letters *b* and *s*
3. To practice problem-solving skills
4. To identify the beginning sounds of a word

RELATED CURRICULUM THEMES:

Sports	Colors	Sounds
Seasons	Occupations	Exercise
Health	Things in My World	Safety

DIRECTIONS:

1. Print the title Do the objects begin with a b or an s? across the top of a piece of tagboard. (*See photograph.*)
2. Divide the remainder of the tagboard into six equal sections.
3. Draw or paste an object that begins with the letter *b* or *s* in each space.
4. Draw a line under each object.
5. Cover the chart with clear Con-Tact paper or laminate it.

TOOLS AND ACCESSORIES:

- Watercolor markers
- Crayons
- Grease pencil
- Damp cloth/sponge
- Laminated alphabet cards
- Object words written on cards and laminated

VARIATIONS AND EXTENSIONS:

1. Prepare charts for other alphabet letters.
2. Provide a word card with the name printed for the six objects.
3. Make a chart using theme-related objects.

FLOWER/LETTER MATCH

DEVELOPMENTAL GOALS:

1. To match uppercase and lowercase letters
2. To develop visual discrimination skills
3. To develop problem-solving skills
4. To develop eye–hand coordination skills
5. To develop small-muscle coordination skills

RELATED CURRICULUM THEMES:

Alphabet Letters   Communication   Spring

Flowers   Writing   Plants

DIRECTIONS:

1. Select a colorful piece of tagboard.
2. Draw and cut nine flowers from construction paper or purchase stationery such as that used in the photograph. (*See photograph.*)
3. Draw and cut nine smaller flowers from construction paper or purchase stationery.
4. Mount the smaller flowers on construction paper and cut around the shape.
5. Print an uppercase letter on each flower on the chart.
6. Print a matching lowercase letter on each smaller flower.
7. Mount the large flower pieces on a chart and cover with clear Con-Tact paper or laminate it.

TOOLS AND ACCESSORIES:

- Watercolor markers
- Crayons
- Grease pencil
- Damp cloth/sponge

VARIATIONS AND EXTENSIONS:

1. Change the alphabet letters.
2. Print simple, three-letter words on the flowers, such as can, fan, man, pan, ran, bit, sit, pit, fit.

MAIL

DEVELOPMENTAL GOALS:

1. To practice forming letters
2. To communicate in writing
3. To develop an appreciation for the printed word
4. To practice addressing an envelope

5. To recognize one's own name as well as those of other people within their social environment
6. To learn where the stamp, return address, and address are placed on an envelope

RELATED CURRICULUM THEMES:

Writing	Writing Tools	Mail Carriers
Numbers	Shapes	The Post Office
Holidays	I'm Me. I'm Special	Occupations
Families	Containers	Valentine's Day

DIRECTIONS:

1. Cut a piece of tagboard into an eight-by-thirteen-inch rectangle.
2. Print a return address in the upper right corner.
3. Draw and color a stamp in the upper right corner.
4. Cut and attach a piece of manuscript paper (or provide lines) for the address. (*See photograph.*)
5. Cover the finished piece with clear Con-Tact paper or laminate it.

TOOLS AND ACCESSORIES:

- Watercolor markers
- Crayons
- Grease pencil
- Damp cloth/sponge

VARIATIONS AND EXTENSIONS:

1. Print the names and addresses of all the children in the class. The children can practice writing their friends' names and addresses.
2. Let the children create a bulletin board by posting their envelopes. Cut out a caption—Our Addresses.

MISSING LETTERS

Missing Letters

Look at the picture.
Look at the word.
Fill in the missing letters.

1. g _ _ _

2. _ u _

3. _ _ t

4. _ _ _ _ w _ _

cup   cat
flower   gift

DEVELOPMENTAL GOALS:

1. To identify the missing letters in words
2. To develop an appreciation for the printed word
3. To develop visual discrimination skills
4. To develop problem-solving skills
5. To develop eye–hand coordination skills
6. To practice forming letters
7. To develop small-muscle coordination skills

RELATED CURRICULUM THEMES:

Alphabet

Symbols

Writing

Reading

Communication

Our World

DIRECTIONS:

1. Across the top of a piece of tagboard, print the title Missing Letters.
2. Print the directions:
   Look at the picture.
   Look at the word.
   Fill in the missing letters.
3. Print the numeral 1. Next to it, draw a gift box. (*See photograph.*) Print the letter *g*. Then draw three short lines for the missing letters in the word.
4. Print the numeral 2. Next to it, draw a cup. Draw a short line for the first letter. Then print the letter *u*, followed by another short line.
5. Print the numeral 3. Next to it, draw a cat face. Draw two short lines, and then print the letter *t*.
6. Print the numeral 4. Next to it, draw a flower. Draw three short lines, print the letter *w*, and draw another short line.
7. Print the words cup, cake, flower, and gift on the bottom of the chart.
8. Create appeal by adding color to the gift, cup, cat, and flower.
9. Cover the finished piece with clear Con-Tact paper or laminate it.

TOOLS AND ACCESSORIES:

- Watercolor markers
- Crayons
- Grease pencil
- Damp cloth/sponge

VARIATIONS AND EXTENSIONS:

Similar teacher-made materials can be adapted to any curriculum theme.

MORE MISSING LETTERS

More Missing Letters

Look at the picture. Then fill in the missing letters.

1. c _ _

2. _ _ t

3. _ _ m _

4. _ _ _ _ _ _ w

pillow   cap

lamp   hat

DEVELOPMENTAL GOALS:

1. To identify the missing letters in words
2. To develop an appreciation for the printed word
3. To develop visual discrimination skills
4. To develop problem-solving skills
5. To develop eye–hand coordination skills
6. To practice forming letters
7. To develop small-muscle coordination skills

RELATED CURRICULUM THEMES:

Alphabet

My World

Writing

Reading

Communication

Symbols

DIRECTIONS:

1. Across the top of a piece of tagboard, print the title More Missing Letters.
2. Print the directions:
   Look at the picture.
   Then fill in the missing letters.
3. Print the numeral 1. Next to it, draw a cap. (*See photograph.*) Then print the letter *c*, followed by two short lines for the missing letters.
4. Print the numeral 2. Next to it, draw a hat followed by two short lines. Then print the letter *t*.
5. Print the numeral 3. Next to it, draw a lamp. Draw two short lines, followed by the letter M and another short line.
6. Print the numeral 4. Next to it, draw a pillow. Draw five short lines, followed by the letter *w*.
7. Create appeal by adding color to the cap, hat, lamp, and pillow.
8. Print the words pillow, cap, lamp, and hat on the bottom of the chart.
9. Cover the finished piece with clear Con-Tact paper or laminate it.

TOOLS AND ACCESSORIES:

- Watercolor markers
- Crayons
- Grease pencil
- Damp cloth/sponge

VARIATIONS AND EXTENSIONS:

1. Similar teacher-made materials can be adapted to any curriculum theme.

MUSICAL INSTRUMENTS

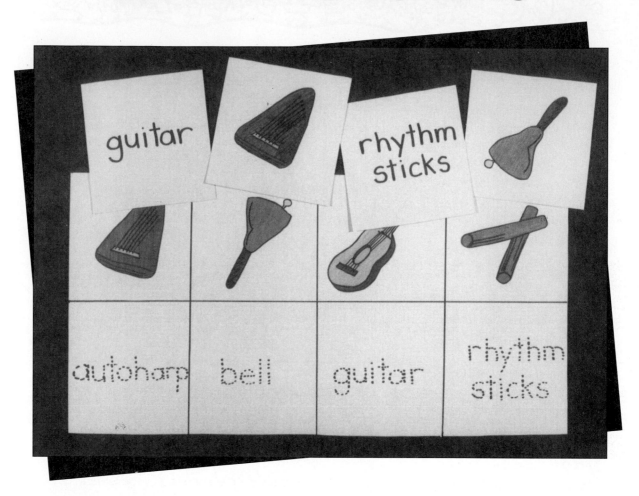

DEVELOPMENTAL GOALS:

1. To associate the printed name of a musical instrument with the object itself
2. To develop an appreciation for the printed word
3. To develop visual discrimination skills
4. To develop problem-solving skills
5. To develop eye–hand coordination skills
6. To practice forming letters and numerals
7. To develop small muscle coordination skills

RELATED CURRICULUM THEMES:

Sound

Entertainment

Music

Communication

Our World

Movement

DIRECTIONS:

1. Cut two 11- × 22-inch inch pieces of tagboard.
2. Divide each piece of tagboard into eight equal sections.
3. Sketch a musical instrument in each box: an autoharp, a bell, a guitar, and a pair of rhythm sticks. (*See photograph.*)
4. Add color and details to the objects.
5. Use broken lines to print the name of each instrument in the box directly under it.
6. Cover the finished piece with clear Con-Tact paper or laminate it.

TOOLS AND ACCESSORIES:

- Watercolor markers
- Crayons
- Grease pencil
- Damp cloth/sponge

VARIATIONS AND EXTENSIONS:

1. Make the material culturally diverse by including other instruments.
2. Extend the variety of instruments.

PLACE SETTINGS

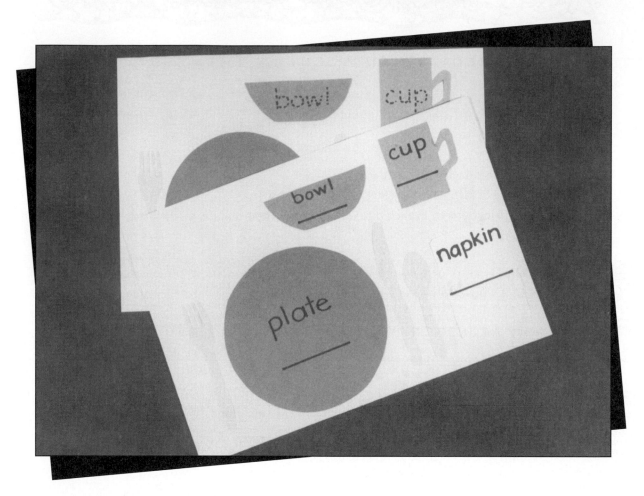

DEVELOPMENTAL GOALS:

1. To practice communicating in writing

2. To develop an appreciation for the printed word

3. To practice forming letters

4. To develop eye–hand coordination skills

RELATED CURRICULUM THEMES:

Families	Health	Shapes
Colors	Nutrition	Meals
All About Me	Foods	Cooking

DIRECTIONS:

1. Select a large piece of colored construction paper to represent a place mat.
2. Using contrasting construction paper, cut out a plate, bowl, cup, knife, fork, spoon, and napkin.
3. Glue the place setting onto the place mat.
4. Print the name of each item on it. (*See photograph.*)
5. Cover the finished piece with clear Con-Tact paper or laminate it.

TOOLS AND ACCESSORIES:

- Watercolor markers
- Crayons
- Grease pencil
- Damp cloth/sponge

VARIATIONS AND EXTENSIONS:

1. Encourage the children to trace over the letters.
2. Prepare a second set of place mats without the words. The children use the first set as a model.
3. Provide materials for children to construct their own place mats.

Sandpaper Alphabet

DEVELOPMENTAL GOALS:

1. To differentiate between uppercase and lowercase letters

2. To tactilely trace the shape of letters

3. To reproduce letters using a writing tool and paper

RELATED CURRICULUM THEMES:

Art

Sounds

Homes

Tools

Occupations

Construction Tools

We Create

Carpenters

Senses

Safety

Scissors

Letters

DIRECTIONS:

1. Cut out fifty-two five-inch squares from tagboard sheets.

2. Using the uppercase and lowercase letter stencils in the Appendix, cut letters out of sandpaper.

3. Attach each sandpaper letter to a tagboard square with rubber cement or glue.

TOOLS AND ACCESSORIES:

• Typing paper—white or colored

• Crayons

• Pencils

VARIATIONS AND EXTENSIONS:

1. The children can feel or trace the letters with their fingers.

2. The children can place a sheet of paper over the square and rub the surface using a pencil or crayon.

TODAY'S WEATHER IS . . .

Today's weather is:

sunny   yes   no

raining   yes   no

snowy   yes   no

DEVELOPMENTAL GOALS:

1. To practice forming letters
2. To practice problem-solving skills
3. To develop concept weather condition
4. To develop visual discrimination skills
5. To communicate in writing
6. To develop an appreciation for the printed word

RELATED CURRICULUM THEMES:

Science

Clothing

Weather

Seasons

Writing

Symbols

DIRECTIONS:

1. On a sheet of tagboard, use a wide felt-tip marker to print the title Today's weather is.
2. Draw the corresponding illustration, using a pencil with soft lead. (*See photograph.*)
3. Draw a picture of the sun, rain, and a snowman using a felt-tipped marker.
4. Under each symbol print the corresponding word.
5. Using a broken line print yes and no behind each weather symbol.
6. Use crayons or colored markers to outline and color the weather symbols.
7. Cover the chart with clear Con-Tact paper or laminate it.

TOOLS AND ACCESSORIES:

- Watercolor markers
- Damp cloth/sponge
- Extra set of six plain laminated cards

VARIATIONS AND EXTENSIONS:

1. Using contrasting watercolor markers, the children could trace over the Yes or No.
2. On separate cards, the children could print Yes or No and attach to the chart.

UPPERCASE BOOK/ LOWERCASE BOOK

DEVELOPMENTAL GOALS:

1. To practice forming alphabet letters
2. To communicate in writing
3. To develop an appreciation for the printed word
4. To develop eye–hand coordination skills
5. To develop small-muscle coordination skills

RELATED CURRICULUM THEMES:

Letters   Writing Tools   Writing Surfaces
Communication   Books   Symbols

DIRECTIONS:

1. Cut tagboard into eight-by-ten-inch pieces. For two complete books, you will need 54 pieces.
2. Print the title Uppercase Book on one tagboard piece.
3. Print the title Lowercase Book on another tagboard piece.
4. Print one uppercase or lowercase letter on each remaining piece of tagboard.
5. Cover all pieces with clear Con-Tact paper or laminate them.
6. Bind pages with metal rings (if desired).

TOOLS AND ACCESSORIES:

- Watercolor markers
- Crayons
- Grease pencil
- Chalk
- Colored pencils
- Pens
- Paper
- Cardboard
- Styrofoam
- Chalkboard
- Aluminum foil
- Foil
- Paint and paint brushes

VARIATIONS AND EXTENSIONS:

1. The children could prepare number books.
2. Pictures of items that begin with the corresponding letter could be added for each page.

UPPERCASE/LOWERCASE PATTERNS

DEVELOPMENTAL GOALS:

1. To practice forming letters of the alphabet
2. To communicate in writing
3. To develop eye–hand coordination
4. To develop small muscle coordination skills

RELATED CURRICULUM THEMES:

Communication	Writing Tools	Writing Surfaces
Newspapers	Libraries	We Create

DIRECTIONS:

1. Cut twenty-six eight-by-eight-inch squares from tagboard.
2. Cut out the alphabet letters from the Appendix.
3. Trace a different letter on each piece of tagboard.
4. Using a craft knife, cut out the letters. (*See photograph.*)
5. Cover the letters with clear Con-Tact paper or laminate them.

TOOLS AND ACCESSORIES:

- Watercolor markers
- Crayons
- Damp cloth/sponge

VARIATIONS AND EXTENSIONS:

1. Prepare letter stencils for the children to trace.
2. Provide stencil and paper for the children to prepare own cutout letter.

WORDS I KNOW

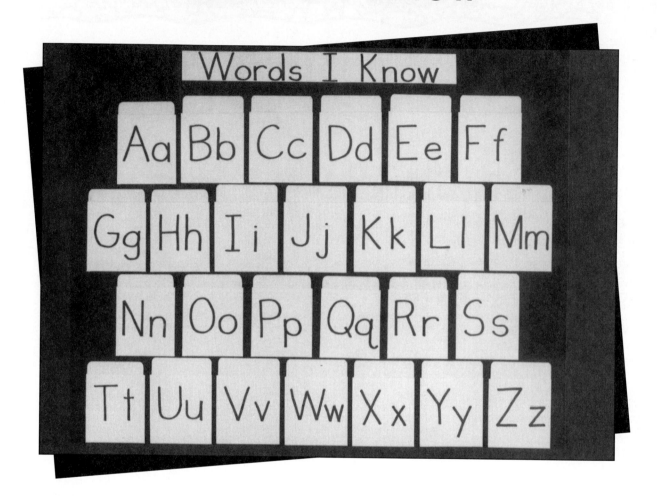

DEVELOPMENTAL GOALS:

1. To develop an appreciation for the printed word
2. To develop visual discrimination skills
3. To develop problem-solving skills
4. To develop eye–hand coordination skills
5. To develop small-muscle coordination skills

RELATED CURRICULUM THEMES:

Words

Alphabet Letters

Writing

Books

Communication

Writing Tools

DIRECTIONS:

1. Paste twenty-four library card pockets on a sheet of tagboard.
2. On a piece of paper, print the title Words I Know. (*See photograph.*)
3. Beginning with the letter A, print the uppercase letters on cards.
4. Cover the chart with clear Con-Tact paper or laminate.
5. Use a craft knife or scissor blade to slit pocket opening.
6. Provide three-by-five-inch index cards for children to write words on.
7. Encourage the children to sort their index cards into the appropriate pockets.

TOOLS AND ACCESSORIES:

- Watercolor markers
- Crayons
- Grease pencil
- Damp cloth/sponge
- Index cards

VARIATIONS AND EXTENSIONS:

1. A chart could be constructed for each child, or children could make their own charts.
2. The chart could be adapted by converting it for word families. Include pockets for *at*, *it*, *ite*, *an*, and *ook*.

CHAPTER 4

BEGINNING SOUNDS • FIRE FIGHTERS • LETTER SOUNDS • RHYME BOARDS • RHYMING WORD CARDS • WORD FAMILIES • TOYS

BEGINNING SOUNDS

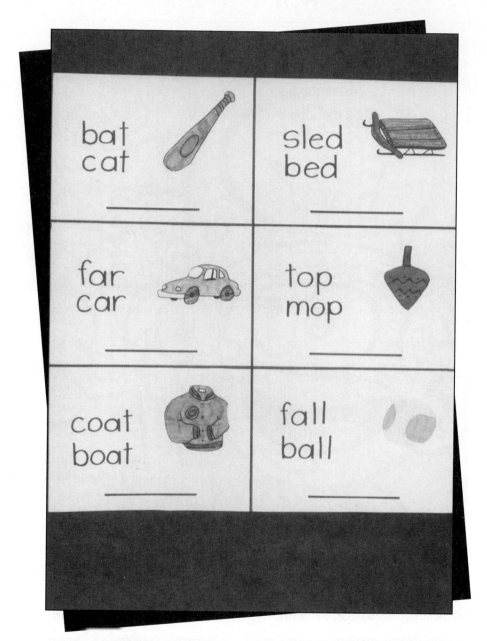

bat cat _____	sled bed _____
far car _____	top mop _____
coat boat _____	fall ball _____

DEVELOPMENTAL GOALS:

1. To identify the beginning sounds of words
2. To practice forming alphabet-letter skills
3. To match the printed word with an object
4. To develop an appreciation for the printed word
5. To communicate in writing
6. To develop eye–hand coordination skills

RELATED CURRICULUM THEMES:

Rhyming Words	Clothing	Toys
Weather	Cars	Wheels
Games	Transportation	Travel
Sounds	Occupations	Seasons

DIRECTIONS:

1. Divide a piece of tagboard into six equal sections
2. Draw or paste a symbol in each section. (*See photograph.*)
3. If the object is drawn, color it to add interest.
4. Print two words in each box. One word must be the name of the object.
5. Draw a line at the bottom of the box.
6. Cover the chart with clear Con-Tact paper or laminate it.

TOOLS AND ACCESSORIES:

- Watercolor markers
- Crayons
- Grease pencil
- Damp cloth/sponge
- Index cards (tagboard)

VARIATIONS AND EXTENSIONS:

1. Prepare charts using objects related to the curriculum theme.
2. Provide materials for the children to make their own charts.

Fire Fighters

DEVELOPMENTAL GOALS:

1. To associate the printed word with an object
2. To practice forming letters
3. To develop eye-hand coordination skills
4. To develop an appreciation for the printed word
5. To communicate by writing

RELATED CURRICULUM THEMES:

Community Helpers   Fire Fighters   Occupations

Safety   Tools   Words

DIRECTIONS:

1. Cut a twelve-by-twenty-inch piece of tagboard.
2. Divide the tagboard into eight four-by-five-inch sections. (*See photograph.*)
3. Draw an object in each of the four top boxes: a ladder, hose, fire truck, and fire fighter.
4. Print, using broken lines, the name of each item in the box directly under it.
5. Color the objects with felt-tip markers.
6. Add detail by outlining objects with a black felt-tip marker.
7. Cut four four-by-five-inch cards. Draw identical objects on each, adding color and detail. Print the name of the object on the reverse side.
8. Cover tagboard with clear Con-Tact paper or laminate.

TOOLS AND ACCESSORIES:

- Watercolor markers
- Damp cloth/sponge

VARIATIONS AND EXTENSIONS:

1. This activity could be extended to any curriculum theme by substituting other sets of related objects.
2. If developmentally appropriate, omit the names of the objects. Instead, provide a line for the children to write them in.

LETTER SOUNDS

DEVELOPMENTAL GOALS:

1. To associate the beginning sound of an object
2. To develop visual discrimination skills
3. To develop problem-solving skills
4. To develop eye–hand coordination skills
5. To practice forming letters and numerals
6. To develop small-muscle coordination skills

RELATED CURRICULUM THEMES:

Words

Sounds

Communication

Symbols

Letters

Writing

DIRECTIONS:

1. Across the top of a piece of tagboard, print Beginning Sounds.
2. Print a *b* next to the title.
3. Draw a ball as an example of the *b* sound next to the letter. (*See photograph.*)
4. Draw a horizontal line below the title.
5. Divide the remaining tagboard into twelve equal sections using a ruler and marker.
6. Draw objects in each of the sections, providing six objects that begin with the letter *b*.
7. Color the objects with CRAY-PAS or felt-tip markers to add interest.
8. Next to each object, draw a line on which the children can print the first letter of the word.
9. Cover the chart with clear Con-Tact paper or laminate it.

TOOLS AND ACCESSORIES:

- Watercolor markers
- Crayons
- Grease pencil
- Damp cloth/sponge

VARIATIONS AND EXTENSIONS:

1. Construct individual beginning-sound sheets.
2. Once the children have mastered beginning sounds, they could print the entire word for the object pictured.

RHYME BOARDS

DEVELOPMENTAL GOALS:

1. To associate a printed word with an object
2. To develop an appreciation for the printed word
3. To practice forming letters
4. To develop eye–hand coordination skills
5. To develop small-muscle coordination skills

RELATED CURRICULUM THEMES:

Sounds	Communication	Things in My World
Animals	Tools	Clothes
Toys	Writing	Letters

DIRECTIONS:

1. Select a piece of tagboard.
2. Divide and cut the piece of tagboard into four sections.
3. Using a felt-tip marker, divide another tagboard sheet into quarters. (*See photograph*.)
4. Select rhyming object words. Draw or paste objects on the pieces of tagboard and the sheet that was divided into quarters. Examples include:

   - hat
   - rat
   - snail
   - man
   - dog
   - bat
   - pail
   - mail
   - fan
   - log
   - cat
   - nail
   - can
   - pan
   - hog

5. Draw a line under each object.
6. Cover with clear Con-Tact paper or laminate.

TOOLS AND ACCESSORIES:

- Watercolor markers
- Crayons
- Damp cloth/sponge

VARIATIONS AND EXTENSIONS:

1. Make a chart including the names of all objects that were used for the rhyme board.
2. If developmentally appropriate, print under each item all the letters but the last one—the ending sound. Provide a space for it.

RHYMING WORD CARDS

ring
ring

swing
swing

can
can

man
man

pan
pan

fan
fan

car
car

star
star

bat
bat

cat
cat

dog
dog

log
log

fish
fish

dish
dish

DEVELOPMENTAL GOALS:

1. To associate a printed word with an object
2. To practice forming letters
3. To develop eye–hand coordination skills
4. To develop an appreciation for the printed word
5. To communicate in writing
6. To develop an awareness of rhyming words

RELATED CURRICULUM THEMES:

Rhymes

Communication

Writing

Sounds

Letters

Things In My World

DIRECTIONS:

1. Divide a piece of tagboard horizontally into seven equal sections. (*See photograph.*)
2. Draw or paste an item on the left side of the row and an item that rhymes with it on the right side. Continue until rows are complete.
3. Print the name of the item under the item. Repeat using broken-line printing.
4. Cover the chart with clear Con-Tact paper or laminate it.

TOOLS AND ACCESSORIES:

- Watercolor markers
- Crayons
- Grease pencil
- Damp cloth/sponge

VARIATIONS AND EXTENSIONS:

1. Make an identical chart, but do not include the names of the items. Instead, make separate name cards for the children to sort.
2. Create word charts for the various word families, such as: *at*, *it*, *an*, and *ing*.

WORD FAMILIES

DEVELOPMENTAL GOALS:

1. To become aware of word sounds
2. To communicate through the printed word
3. To explore letter combinations
4. To practice forming letters
5. To develop word association
6. To develop visual discrimination skills
7. To develop small-muscle coordination skills.

RELATED CURRICULUM THEMES:

Communication

Toys

Farm Animals

Mail Carrier

Homes

Transportation

Construction Tools

Seasons

Water

Sports

Beaches/Soil

DIRECTIONS:

1. Choose a piece of white or colored tagboard.
2. Print the title Word Families across the top of the tagboard. (*See photograph*.).
3. Draw a line under the title. Then divide the remainder of the board into six squares.
4. In each square, place a picture that has been drawn or cut from a magazine.
5. Under each picture, draw a short line for the first letter of the word. Print the remaining letters of the word.
6. Cover the chart with clear Con-Tact paper or laminate it.

VARIATIONS AND EXTENSIONS:

1. The children could print the missing letter in the blank space.
2. The children could look at the pictures and sound out the words. Ask: "What sound is first?" "What letter makes that sound?" "What letter do you think it is?"
3. The children could copy the entire word below the one that is already printed in the square.
4. Alphabet cards or vinyl letters could be looked at, sounded out, and placed in the appropriate spaces.

5. Ask: "What other words could we make using the *ail* sound?" (hail, jail, and so on.)
6. Similar charts can be prepared for other word families.

TOOLS AND ACCESSORIES:

- Watercolor markers
- Crayons
- Grease pencil
- Damp cloth/sponge

Toys

DEVELOPMENTAL GOALS:

1. To associate a printed word with an object
2. To develop visual discrimination skills
3. To develop problem-solving skills
4. To develop language skills
5. To develop an appreciation for the printed word
6. To communicate in writing

RELATED CURRICULUM THEMES:

Things I Like

Words

Friends

Colors

Letters

Toys

Sounds

Sports

Wheels

DIRECTIONS:

1. Select a piece of white or colored tagboard.
2. Print the word Toys across the top of the paper.
3. Under the title, draw a line and then divide the remainder of the paper into nine squares.
4. Draw nine different items to place on squares of construction paper. Stickers, coloring-book or magazine pictures also could be used.
5. Glue one object in each box.
6. Under each picture, print three words. One word must name the object in the picture.
7. Cover the chart with clear Con-Tact paper or laminate it.

TOOLS AND ACCESSORIES:

- Watercolor markers
- Crayons
- Grease pencil
- Damp cloth/sponge

VARIATIONS AND EXTENSIONS:

When the children can distinguish between beginning sounds, change the words. Provide words that begin with the same letter to make the activity more challenging.

CHAPTER 5

BIRTHDAY CAKE • CHRISTMAS TREE • EASTER BASKET • MAKE A
HALLOWEEN CARD • MAKE A VALENTINE • VALENTINE ALPHABET •
VALENTINE SORT • VALENTINE WORDS • VALENTINE NUMBERS

BIRTHDAY CAKE

DEVELOPMENTAL GOALS:

1. To associate the name of a color with the printed word

2. To develop an appreciation for the printed word

3. To develop visual discrimination skills

4. To develop eye–hand coordination skills

5. To practice forming letters

6. To develop small-muscle coordination skills

RELATED CURRICULUM THEMES:

My World

Celebrations

Holidays

Colors

Communications

Foods

DIRECTIONS:

1. Sketch a cake on a large piece of tagboard and then cut it out. (*See photograph*.)
2. Use a CRAY-PAS color or felt-tip marker to make the cake appear layered. Make a horizontal slit with a craft knife in the top section of the tagboard cake.
3. Using rubber cement, attach a piece of aluminum foil to represent a plate.
4. Make candles from green, yellow, red, purple, pink, and blue construction paper.
5. Sketch, cut and glue a yellow flame on each candle.
6. Print, using a broken line, the color name on each candle.
7. Cover the finished piece with clear Con-Tact paper or laminate it.
8. Use a craft knife to open slit in top section of the cake.

TOOLS AND ACCESSORIES:

- Watercolor markers
- Crayons
- Grease pencil
- Damp cloth/sponge

VARIATIONS AND EXTENSIONS:

If developmentally appropriate, use other colors such as gray, aqua, magenta, orange, rose, and so on.

CHRISTMAS TREE

purple

orange

blue

green

red

yellow

DEVELOPMENTAL GOALS:

1. To identify color words
2. To develop an appreciation of the printed word
3. To communicate by writing
4. To practice forming letters
5. To develop small-muscle coordination skills

RELATED CURRICULUM THEMES:

Christmas

Holidays

Symbols

Shapes

Colors

Trees

DIRECTIONS:

1. Cut a tree from a large piece of green tagboard. (*See photograph.*)
2. Cut a stand from a piece of brown construction paper, and glue it to the bottom of the tree.
3. Add detail by tracing around the edges of the tree with a darker colored felt-tip marker and around the edges of the stand with a brown marker.
4. Cut large circles from a variety of colors of construction paper.
5. Print, using a broken line, the name of the color of each circle.
6. Cover the finished piece with clear Con-Tact paper or laminate it.

TOOLS AND ACCESSORIES:

- Watercolor markers
- Crayons
- Tape or glue
- Damp cloth/sponge

VARIATIONS AND EXTENSIONS:

1. The children could decorate the ornament after printing the color word.
2. The children could create ornaments using several colors. On the reverse side, the names of the colors used could be printed.

EASTER BASKET

DEVELOPMENTAL GOALS:

1. To practice forming alphabet letters
2. To identify color words
3. To develop an appreciation for the printed word

4. To develop visual discrimination skills
5. To develop eye–hand coordination skills
6. To develop small-muscle coordination skills

RELATED CURRICULUM THEMES:

Holidays

Eggs

Celebrations

Foods

Easter

Baskets

DIRECTIONS:

1. Draw a basket on a large piece of tagboard or construction paper. (*See photograph.*)
2. Use markers or CRAY-PAS to color the basket and bow.
3. Outline the basket and add detail using a black felt-tip marker.
4. Cut strips of green construction paper to resemble grass and glue on the basket.
5. Cut egg shapes out of colored tagboard or construction paper.
6. Use broken lines to print the corresponding color word on each egg.
7. Cover eggs and basket with clear Con-Tact paper or laminate them.

TOOLS AND ACCESSORIES:

- Watercolor markers
- Crayons
- Grease pencil
- Damp cloth/sponge

VARIATIONS AND EXTENSIONS:

1. A fruit basket could be substituted for the Easter basket.
2. The color of the eggs could be varied.
3. The eggs could be left blank, allowing children to write the color word without assistance.

MAKE A HALLOWEEN CARD

Make a Halloween card.

Have a happy Halloween.

Trick or treat !

Carve a pumpkin.

I like your silly costume.

DEVELOPMENTAL GOALS:

1. To develop an appreciation for the printed word
2. To develop visual discrimination skills
3. To develop problem-solving skills
4. To develop eye–hand coordination skills
5. To practice forming alphabet letters
6. To develop small-muscle coordination skills

RELATED CURRICULUM THEMES:

Halloween

Communication

Holidays

The Alphabet

Our Friends

Writing

DIRECTIONS:

1. Select a black piece of tagboard.
2. Cut five strips of manuscript paper. (*See photograph*.)
3. Print each of the following lines on the manuscript paper:
   Make a Halloween card.
   Have a happy Halloween.
   Trick or treat!
   Carve a pumpkin.
   I like your silly costume.
4. Paste or glue each manuscript strip on individual pieces of orange construction paper that are large enough to leave a one-quarter-inch border.
5. Cut two pumpkins from orange construction paper and add a green stem on each.
6. Paste or glue the pumpkins on the chart.
7. Cover chart with Con-Tact paper or laminate it.

TOOLS AND ACCESSORIES:

- Watercolor markers
- Crayons
- Grease pencil
- Damp cloth/sponge

VARIATIONS AND EXTENSIONS:

1. Charts for cards could be made for Thanksgiving, Christmas, Hanukkah, Valentine's Day, Mother's Day, St. Patrick's Day, Father's Day, Easter, and May Day.
2. Thank-you-card and birthday-card charts also could be made.

MAKE A VALENTINE

Make a valentine.

Happy Valentine's day!

Be my valentine.

You are as sweet as candy.

I want you for my valentine.

I love you.

Have a heart, valentine.

DEVELOPMENTAL GOALS:

1. To make a Valentine by selecting and copying a greeting
2. To develop an appreciation for the printed word
3. To develop visual discrimination skills
4. To develop problem-solving skills
5. To develop eye–hand coordination skills
6. To practice forming alphabet letters
7. To develop small-muscle coordination skills

RELATED CURRICULUM THEMES:

Holidays

Writing

Valentine's Day

Communication

Friends

Symbols

DIRECTIONS:

1. Select a large piece of red or pink tagboard.
2. Print the title Make a valentine on a manuscript strip. (*See photograph.*)
3. Print messages on strips of manuscript. Possibilities include:
   Happy Valentine's Day!
   Be my valentine.
   You are as sweet as candy.
   I want you for my valentine.
   I love you.
   Have a heart, valentine.
4. Glue the strips on the piece of tagboard.
5. Using a black, broad-tipped marker, draw a frame around the tagboard edges.
6. If desired, draw hearts or add some heart stickers.
7. Cover the finished piece with clear Con-Tact paper or laminate it.

TOOLS AND ACCESSORIES:

- Watercolor markers
- Crayons
- Grease pencil
- Damp cloth/sponge

VARIATIONS AND EXTENSIONS:

Similar charts can be made for Easter, Hanukkah, Thanksgiving, Mother's Day, Father's Day, and birthdays.

VALENTINE ALPHABET

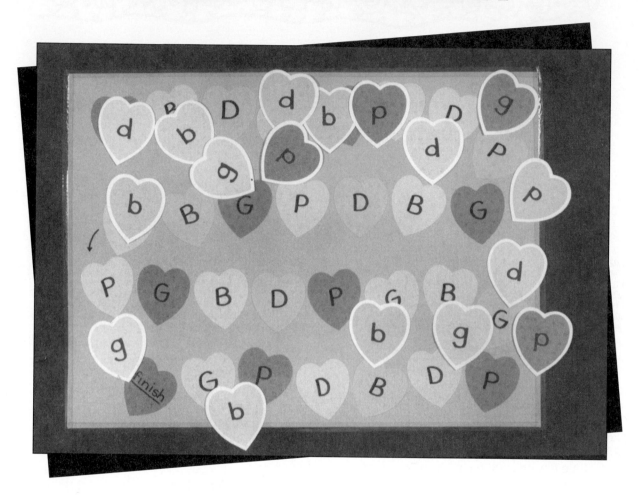

DEVELOPMENTAL GOALS:

1. To recognize uppercase and lowercase letters
2. To match uppercase and lowercase letters
3. To practice problem-solving skills
4. To develop visual discrimination skills

RELATED CURRICULUM THEMES:

Letters

Shapes

Holiday

Writing

Communication

Celebrations

Games

Valentine's Day

Friends

DIRECTIONS:

1. Cut two identical sets of thirty hearts each from colored construction paper. (*See photograph.*)

2. Print sets of uppercase and lowercase letters on 28 of the hearts from each set. Print the word "start" on one of the remaining hearts and "finish" on the other.

3. Glue one set of hearts onto a piece of colorful tagboard paper. The first heart should have the word "start" printed on it. The last heart will have the word "finish" on it.

4. Use a felt-tip marker to show children the playing sequence.

5. Cover the board with clear Con-Tact paper or laminate it.

TOOLS AND ACCESSORIES:

- Watercolor markers
- Crayons
- Grease pencil
- Damp cloth/sponge

VARIATIONS AND EXTENSIONS:

1. Vary the game by using symbols for other holidays.

2. Construct game boards for children to match lowercase to lowercase letters or uppercase to uppercase letters.

VALENTINE SORT

DEVELOPMENTAL GOALS·

1. To develop an understanding of sets
2. To associate the printed word with its numeral
3. To develop eye–hand coordination skills
4. To associate symbols with celebrated occasions
5. To review the heart shape

RELATED CURRICULUM THEMES:

Communication	Writing	Feelings
Numbers	Friends	Letters
Valentine's Day	Colors	Hearts

DIRECTIONS:

1. Cut a large heart from a piece of red tagboard.
2. If desired, add a decorative border around the edge of the heart.
3. Glue pockets to the heart.
4. Cut small hearts from red and pink construction paper.
5. Glue the hearts on the pockets. (*See photograph.*)
6. Print a corresponding numeral and its name under the hearts.
7. Using a broken line, repeat the numeral and its name.
8. Cut larger hearts from tagboard for children to insert in the pockets.
9. Cover the pieces with clear Con-Tact paper or laminate them.

TOOLS AND ACCESSORIES:

- Watercolor markers
- Crayons
- Grease pencil
- Damp cloth/sponge

VARIATIONS AND EXTENSIONS:

1. Depending on the developmental level of the children, vary the numerals.
2. Use the material to create a bulletin board in the classroom.

VALENTINE WORDS

DEVELOPMENTAL GOALS:

1. To identify Valentine's Day words
2. To practice writing the words heart, valentine, love, friend, card, candy, Mom, and Dad
3. To develop an awareness of the printed word
4. To practice eye–hand coordination skills

RELATED CURRICULUM THEMES:

Valentine's Day
Communication

Shapes
Celebrations

Holidays
Friendship

DIRECTIONS:

1. Print the title Valentine Words across the top of a piece of tagboard with a medium felt-tip marker
2. Cut eight large hearts from construction paper, three of them red and five pink. Also cut about a dozen smaller hearts. (*See photograph.*)
3. Glue the hearts onto the tagboard.
4. Cut a piece of manuscript paper to fit on each large heart. If unavailable, prepare a strip by drawing two horizontal lines one inch apart. Measure one-half inch down from the top line and draw a row of broken lines.
5. Glue the strips of manuscript paper onto the hearts.
6. On each piece of manuscript paper, print one word: heart, valentine, love, friend, card, candy, Mom, and Dad.
7. Cover the chart with clear Con-Tact paper or laminate it.

TOOLS AND ACCESSORIES:

- Watercolor markers
- Crayons
- Grease pencil
- Damp cloth/sponge

VARIATIONS AND EXTENSIONS:

1. Provide materials for children to prepare their own word charts.
2. Prepare a chart without the words, and provide word cards that the children can copy onto the chart.

VALENTINE NUMBERS

DEVELOPMENTAL GOALS:

1. To develop an appreciation for the printed word
2. To develop visual discrimination skills
3. To develop problem-solving skills
4. To develop eye–hand coordination skills
5. To practice forming letters and numerals
6. To develop small-muscle coordination skills

RELATED CURRICULUM THEMES:

Holidays   Friends   Writing

Valentine's Day   Shapes   Numbers

DIRECTIONS:

1. Cut ten four-by-twelve-inch pieces of red tagboard.
2. Cut ten three-by-ten-inch strips of manuscript paper or draw lines on beige or white construction paper. (*See photograph.*)
3. Attach stickers or draw hearts on the left side of the manuscript strip.
4. Paste the manuscript paper on the tagboard pieces, allowing for a border on all four sides.
5. Cover the finished pieces with clear Con-Tact paper or laminate them.

TOOLS AND ACCESSORIES:

- Watercolor markers
- Crayons
- Grease pencil
- Damp cloth/sponge

VARIATIONS AND EXTENSIONS:

1. Symbols representing other holidays could be used.
2. Prepare an accompanying chart with words for the numerals 1–10.

CHAPTER 6

A PLAYGROUND • BAKED FOODS • BAKERY SHOP • BREADS • BREAKFAST FOODS • FARM AND ZOO ANIMALS • FRUIT/VEGETABLE WORD CARDS • FOODS THAT GROW ON TREES • HARD OR SOFT? • IS IT WHOLE OR HALF? • BREAKFAST FOODS/LUNCH FOODS • MEAL MENUS • MY GARDEN • PLAYGROUND EQUIPMENT • SETS OF TIES • WHAT'S FOR LUNCH?

A PLAYGROUND

DEVELOPMENTAL GOALS:

1. To associate the printed name with a piece of playground equipment

2. To develop an appreciation for the printed word

3. To develop visual discrimination skills

4. To develop problem-solving skills

5. To develop eye-hand coordination skills

6. To develop small-muscle coordination skills

RELATED CURRICULUM THEMES:

Play	Our School	Communication
Words	The Alphabet	Equipment

DIRECTIONS:

1. Across the top of a piece of green tagboard, print the words slide, sandbox, swings, climber, and seesaw. (*See photograph.*)
2. Cut a fence from brown construction paper.
3. Glue the fence onto the tagboard directly under the names of playground equipment.
4. Draw the playground equipment or cut and paste pieces from a catalog.
5. Add color using markers if objects are hand drawn.
6. Cover the chart with clear Con-Tact paper or laminate it.

TOOLS AND ACCESSORIES:

- Watercolor markers
- Crayons
- Grease pencil
- Damp cloth/sponge

VARIATIONS AND EXTENSIONS:

1. Substitute or add toys such as balls, tricycles, scooters, wagons, and a playhouse.
2. Provide space on the chart for children to write the names of the playground equipment.

Baked Goods

_read

_uffin

_ake

_ortilla

_ita

_agel

_ie

_roissan

_oaf

bread   croissant   pie
bagel   loaf   pita
cake   muffin   tortil

DEVELOPMENTAL GOALS:

1. To identify the names of different types of bread
2. To develop an appreciation for the printed word
3. To communicate in writing
4. To develop eye-hand coordination skills
5. To identify beginning sounds
6. To practice problem-solving skills
7. To develop visual discrimination skills

RELATED CURRICULUM THEMES:

Foods	Celebrations	Health
Baking	Holidays	Breads

DIRECTIONS:

1. Select a piece of tagboard.
2. Divide the tagboard into ten equal sections. (*See photograph*.)
3. Draw or cut and paste a picture in each box. Include bread, a muffin, a cake, a tortilla, pita, a bagel, a pie, a croissant, and a loaf.
4. If necessary, color items using CRAY-PAS or markers. To add detail, use a black felt-tip marker.
5. Cut pieces of manuscript paper two lines wide and paste them next to each item.
6. Draw a short line for the first letter of the object. Then print the remaining letters.
7. In the bottom section of the right side, print the names of all of the items.
8. Cover the chart with clear Con-Tact paper or laminate it.

TOOLS AND ACCESSORIES:

- Watercolor markers
- Crayons
- Grease pencil
- Damp cloth/sponge

VARIATIONS AND EXTENSIONS:

1. Create identical boards for fruits, vegetables, and meats.
2. If developmentally appropriate, make another chart but omit the letters in each word and provide only spaces for them.

BAKERY SHOP

DEVELOPMENTAL GOALS:

1. To associate a printed word with the object
2. To develop an appreciation for the printed word
3. To develop visual discrimination skills
4. To develop problem-solving skills
5. To develop eye-hand coordination skills
6. To practice forming letters
7. To develop small-muscle coordination skills

RELATED CURRICULUM THEMES:

Breads

Foods

Health

Community Helpers

Occupations

Nutrition

DIRECTIONS:

1. Print the title Bakery Shop across the top of a piece of colored tagboard.
2. Sketch a window with nine panes on the tagboard. (*See photograph.*)
3. Sketch a cake, a piece of bread, a loaf of bread, a muffin, a tortilla, a bagel, a croissant, a pie, and pita on light tan or beige construction paper.
4. Add color to the bakery items with CRAY-PAS or felt-tip markers to create interest.
5. Add details with a felt-tip marker.
6. Glue or paste one bakery item in each window pane.
7. Print, using broken lines, the name under each bakery item.
8. Cover the chart with clear Con-Tact paper or laminate it.

TOOLS AND ACCESSORIES:

- Watercolor markers
- Crayons
- Grease pencil
- Damp cloth/sponge

VARIATIONS AND EXTENSIONS:

1. If developmentally appropriate, omit printing the name of the objects.
2. Charts depicting items related to other stores or shops could be constructed.

BREADS

Breads

pie	pita	muffin
croissant	cake	bagel
loaf	tortilla	bread

DEVELOPMENTAL GOALS:

1. To recognize food items that are classified as bread
2. To communicate using a writing tool
3. To develop an appreciation for the printed word
4. To practice forming letters
5. To develop eye-hand coordination skills

RELATED CURRICULUM THEMES:

Health

Seasons

Plants

Safety

Measuring

Occupations

People in My World

Nutrition

Foods I Eat

Shapes

Transportation

My Body

Colors

Holidays

Farms

We Create

Water

DIRECTIONS:

1. Print the word Breads across the top of a sheet of tagboard. (*See photograph.*)
2. Using a ruler and marker, divide the remaining space into nine sections.
3. Draw or cut from a magazine pictures of a pie, pita, a muffin, a croissant, a cake, a bagel, a loaf of bread, a tortilla, and a slice of bread.
4. If pictures are used, paste one in each of the nine squares.
5. Cut from a sheet of manuscript paper two lines to glue under each object.
6. Across the top line of each sheet of paper, print the name of the object.
7. Cover the chart with clear Con-Tact paper or laminate it.

TOOLS AND ACCESSORIES:

- Watercolor markers
- Crayons
- Grease pencil
- Damp cloth/sponge
- Index cards (tagboard)
- Cards that are prewritten with the words on them (for matching)

VARIATIONS AND EXTENSIONS:

1. Encourage the children to use a marker to individually trace the letters.
2. Prepare variations of the chart for tools, fruit, pasta, or meats.

BREAKFAST FOODS

DEVELOPMENTAL GOALS:

1. To identify the beginning letter of the names of breakfast foods
2. To develop an appreciation for the printed word
3. To develop visual discrimination skills
4. To develop problem-solving skills
5. To develop eye-hand coordination skills
6. To practice forming letters
7. To develop small-muscle coordination skills

RELATED CURRICULUM THEMES:

Foods

Holidays

Writing

Nutrition

Health

Meals

DIRECTIONS:

1. Across the top of a sheet of tagboard, print the title Breakfast Foods.
2. Below the title, draw a horizontal line across the tagboard.
3. Divide the remainder of the tagboard into nine sections of equal size.
4. Draw or paste a picture of breakfast foods in each section. (*See photograph.*)
5. Add color using CRAY-PAS or crayons if the pictures are hand drawn. Use a black felt-tip marker to add details.
6. Print the name of each food (omitting the first letter) next to the picture.
7. Cover the finished piece with clear Con-Tact paper or laminate it.

TOOLS AND ACCESSORIES:

- Watercolor markers
- Crayons
- Grease pencil
- Damp cloth/sponge

VARIATIONS AND EXTENSIONS:

1. Make a chart for lunch and dinner foods.
2. Substitute foods of various ethnic origins.

FARM AND ZOO ANIMALS

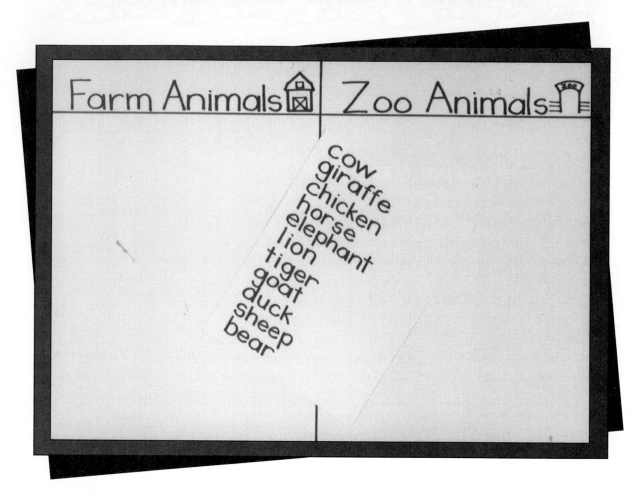

Farm Animals	Zoo Animals

cow
giraffe
chicken
horse
elephant
lion
tiger
goat
duck
sheep
bear

DEVELOPMENTAL GOALS:

1. To distinguish between the written names of farm and zoo animals

2. To develop an appreciation for the printed word

3. To develop visual discrimination skills

4. To develop problem-solving skills

5. To develop eye–hand coordination skills

6. To practice forming letters

7. To develop small-muscle coordination skills

RELATED CURRICULUM THEMES:

Animal Homes

Veterinarian

The Farm

Zoo Animals

Farm Animals

Animals

DIRECTIONS:

1. Divide a piece of tagboard in half vertically, using a felt-tip marker. (*See photograph.*)
2. Across the top, write the words Farm Animals on one side of the line. Write the words Zoo Animals on the other side.
3. Print the names of zoo and farm animals on an 8 1/2-by-11-inch piece of construction paper.
4. Cover both pieces with clear Con-Tact paper or laminate them.

TOOLS AND ACCESSORIES:

- Watercolor markers
- Crayons
- Grease pencil
- Damp cloth/sponge

VARIATIONS AND EXTENSIONS:

1. The names of other animals could be added.
2. Pictures of animals could be glued or drawn next to the written word.

FRUIT/VEGETABLE WORD CARDS

DEVELOPMENTAL GOALS:

1. To associate a word with an object
2. To practice forming alphabet letters
3. To develop fine muscle skills
4. To develop eye-hand coordination skills
5. To develop an appreciation of the printed word

RELATED CURRICULUM THEMES:

Families

Senses

Colors

Nature

Health

Flowers

Seasons

Fruits/Vegetables

Foods

Plants

Shapes

Gardens

DIRECTIONS:

1. On heavy construction paper or tagboard, draw two sets of lines for printing. (*See photograph.*)
2. Draw a fruit or vegetable on the top of each sheet of paper. Magazine pictures may be substituted.
3. Print the name of each item on the top set of lines.
4. Cover the finished pieces with clear Con-Tact paper or laminate them.

TOOLS AND ACCESSORIES:

- Watercolor markers
- Crayons
- Damp cloth/sponge
- Grease pencil

VARIATIONS AND EXTENSIONS:

1. If developmentally appropriate, the children could print the word on the second line.
2. Other objects may be added, such as tomato slices, soup, and sauce.

FOODS THAT GROW ON TREES

Foods that grow on trees

DEVELOPMENTAL GOALS:

1. To identify foods that grow on trees
2. To associate an object with the printed word
3. To practice forming letters
4. To develop eye–hand coordination skills
5. To develop small muscle coordination skills

RELATED CURRICULUM THEMES:

Foods

Fruits

Plants

Colors

Trees

DIRECTIONS:

1. Cut a tree from brown and green construction paper.
2. Glue the tree onto a large piece of tagboard.
3. Outline and add detail to the tree using green and brown felt-tip markers.
4. Print the title Foods that grow on trees across the top or bottom of the piece of tagboard.
5. Draw and cut a walnut, orange, pineapple, apple, and pear from colored construction paper.
6. Add detail to the fruit with a felt-tip marker.
7. Print, using a broken line, the name of each fruit on it. (*See photograph.*)
8. Cover all pieces with clear Con-Tact paper or laminate them.

TOOLS AND ACCESSORIES:

- Grease pencil
- Piece of flannel
- Watercolor markers
- Damp cloth/sponge

VARIATIONS AND EXTENSIONS:

1. Expand the material to include lemons, tangerines, coconuts, mangos, oranges, and grapefruit.
2. If developmentally appropriate, provide a space for the children to write the names of foods that grow on trees.
3. Charts could be prepared for foods grown in the sea, foods grown in the ground, and foods grown in greenhouses.

HARD OR SOFT?

Are the items hard or soft?

diaper	hard soft	high chair	hard soft
rattle	hard soft	blanket	hard soft
bib	hard soft	stroller	hard soft
bottle	hard soft	teddy bear	hard soft

DEVELOPMENTAL GOALS:

1. To distinguish between items that are soft and hard
2. To practice forming letters
3. To communicate in writing
4. To develop eye-hand coordination skills
5. To develop an appreciation for the printed word
6. To develop small muscle coordination skills

RELATED CURRICULUM THEMES:

Clothing

Safety

My Toys

Babies

Homes

All About Me

Families

Toys

Opposites

DIRECTIONS:

1. Print the title Are the items hard or soft? across the top of a piece of tagboard. (*See photograph.*)
2. Draw a horizontal line one inch under the title with a felt-tip marker.
3. Divide the remainder of the tagboard piece into eight blocks.
4. In each block, draw or paste a picture depicting something that is hard or soft.
5. If drawn, color in the item and outline with a felt-tip marker.
6. Using broken lines, print the word "hard" and "soft" in each box.
7. Cover chart with clear Con-Tact paper or laminate it.

TOOLS AND ACCESSORIES:

- Watercolor markers
- Crayons
- Grease pencil
- Damp cloth/sponge

VARIATIONS AND EXTENSIONS:

Charts can be made for other opposites, such as up/down, over/under, inside/outside, hot/cold, big/small, and happy/sad.

IS IT WHOLE OR HALF?

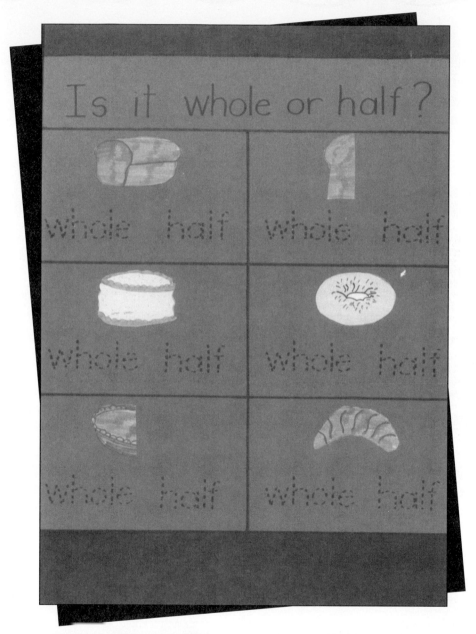

DEVELOPMENTAL GOALS:

1. To develop an understanding of the concepts whole and half
2. To develop problem-solving skills
3. To develop eye-hand coordination skills
4. To practice forming letters
5. To develop visual discrimination skills

RELATED CURRICULUM THEMES:

Words

Foods

Holidays

Celebrations

Fractions

Breads

DIRECTIONS:

1. Print the title Is it whole or half? across the top of a piece of tagboard. (*See photograph.*)
2. Draw a horizontal line with a felt-tip marker one inch under the title.
3. Divide the remainder of the chart into six sections.
4. Draw or paste an object, either whole or half, in each section.
5. Print the words "whole" and "half" under each object.
6. Cover the chart with clear Con-Tact paper or laminate it.

TOOLS AND ACCESSORIES:

- Watercolor markers
- Damp cloth/sponge

VARIATIONS AND EXTENSIONS:

1. Use stickers to make the poster.
2. Construct another poster and write only one word in each section. The children can draw the object.

BREAKFAST FOODS/LUNCH FOODS

DEVELOPMENTAL GOALS:

1. To practice forming letters
2. To develop eye-hand coordination skills
3. To practice small-muscle coordination skills
4. To develop an appreciation for the printed word

RELATED CURRICULUM THEMES:

Communication	Dentist	Doctor
Numbers	Restaurants	Safety
Seasons	Feelings	Foods
Health	Occupations	Meals
Cooking	Holidays	Colors

DIRECTIONS:

1. Select a sheet of colored construction paper or tagboard.
2. Use a felt-tip marker to print the title Breakfast foods/lunch foods across the top of the sheet.
3. Draw or cut and paste pictures of breakfast or lunch foods. (See *photograph*.)
4. Print, using a felt-tip marker and broken lines, the name of each food next to the illustration.
5. Cover the finished piece with clear Con-Tact paper or laminate it.

TOOLS AND ACCESSORIES:

- Watercolor markers
- Crayons
- Grease pencil
- Damp cloth/sponge

VARIATIONS AND EXTENSIONS:

1. Encourage the children to print the word of the food item on the line.
2. Encourage the children to write the word.
3. Construct a chart of foods served at picnics and/or lunches.

MEAL MENUS

DEVELOPMENTAL GOALS:

1. To practice writing the names of breakfast and/or dinner foods

2. To practice forming letters

3. To develop an appreciation for the printed word

4. To improve fine muscle coordination skills

5. To identify nutritious foods

RELATED CURRICULUM THEMES:

Meals	Foods	Families
Farm Animals	Health/Nutrition	Plants
Cooking	Gardens	Senses

DIRECTIONS:

1. Select a piece of colored tagboard. On it, use a felt-tip marker to print the title Breakfast Menu or Dinner Menu.
2. Cut pictures of nutritional breakfast or dinner foods from magazines.
3. Paste the pictures vertically down the left side of the tagboard. (*See photograph*.)
4. Draw a horizontal line with a felt-tip marker next to each picture.
5. Cover chart with clear Con-Tact paper or laminate it.

TOOLS AND ACCESSORIES:

- Watercolor markers
- Crayons
- Damp cloth/sponge
- Grease pencil

VARIATIONS AND EXTENSIONS:

1. Print, using broken lines, the name of each food item next to it.
2. Make food charts for breakfast, lunch, dinner, and snack.

MY GARDEN

DEVELOPMENTAL GOALS:

1. To identify foods that are grown in a garden
2. To identify food words
3. To practice forming letters
4. To develop eye–hand coordination skills
5. To communicate in writing

RELATED CURRICULUM THEMES:

Farms	Fruits/Vegetables	Homes
Plants	Numbers	Gardens
Writing	Spring/Summer/Fall	Health
My Body	Colors	Occupations
Weather	Drawing Tools	My Senses

DIRECTIONS:

1. Select a large piece of colored tagboard.
2. Write the title My garden across the top of the tagboard.
3. Draw three garden rows on the tagboard. (*See photograph.*)
4. Draw and cut three carrots, three potatoes, and three tomatoes out of colored construction paper.
5. Color and add detail to the vegetables, as desired.
6. Print the name on each of the vegetables.
7. Use broken lines to print the names on another set.
8. Draw a line on the remaining vegetables.
9. Cover the chart and the pieces with clear Con-Tact paper or laminate them.
10. Use a craft knife to make slits in the garden rows.

TOOLS AND ACCESSORIES:

- Watercolor markers
- Crayons
- Grease pencil
- Damp cloth/sponge

VARIATIONS AND EXTENSIONS:

1. Extend the activity by providing row markers for other vegetables.

PLAYGROUND EQUIPMENT

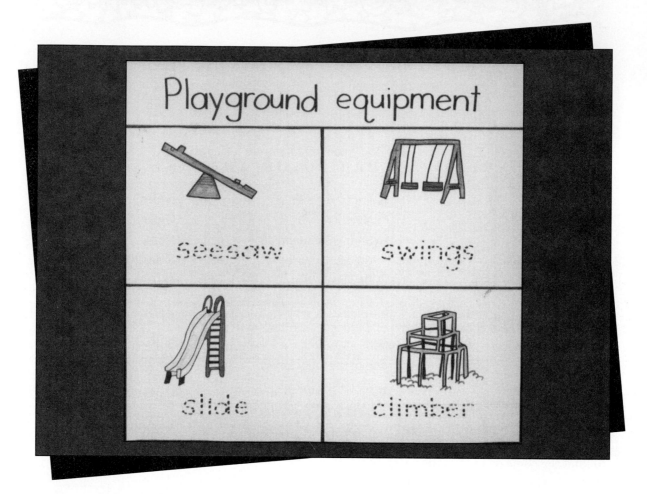

DEVELOPMENTAL GOALS:

1. To associate playground objects with the printed word

2. To practice forming letters

3. To develop an appreciation for the printed word

4. To develop small-muscle skills

5. To communicate by writing

RELATED CURRICULUM THEMES:

Friends

Safety

Weather

Exercise

Movement

Play Yards

DIRECTIONS:

1. Print the title Playground equipment across the top of a piece of tagboard. (*See photograph.*)
2. Using a pencil and ruler, divide the remainder of the tagboard into four equal sections.
3. Trace over the pencil lines with a medium felt-tip marker.
4. Draw one piece of playground equipment in each of the four sections.
5. Print, using broken lines, its name under each piece of equipment.
6. Cover the finished piece with clear Con-Tact paper or laminate it.

TOOLS AND ACCESSORIES:

- Watercolor markers
- Crayons
- Grease pencil
- Damp cloth/sponge

VARIATIONS AND EXTENSIONS:

1. Prepare a set of cards that match the printed words. The children can match the cards to the chart.
2. Prepare additional charts with other playground equipment or adapt the chart to the classroom curriculum theme.

SETS OF TIES

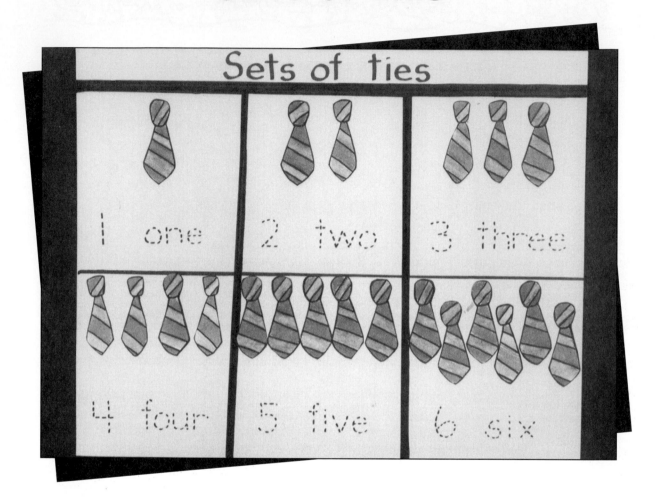

DEVELOPMENTAL GOALS·

1. To associate written numerals with sets of ties
2. To communicate in writing
3. To practice forming letters
4. To distinguish between a numeral and the written word
5. To develop eye–hand coordination skills

RELATED CURRICULUM THEMES:

Clothing   Occupations   Clowns

Colors   Community Helpers   People in My World

DIRECTIONS:

1. Select a sheet of colored tagboard.
2. Print the title Sets of ties across the top of the tagboard with a broad felt-tip marker.
3. Divide the remainder of the tagboard into six equal sections. (*See photograph.*)
4. Draw one tie in the first box, two ties in the second box, and so on.
5. Draw stripes on the ties.
6. Outline the ties with a fine-point felt-tip marker.
7. Print, using broken lines, the appropriate numeral and word in each box.
8. Cover the chart with clear Con-Tact paper or laminate it.

TOOLS AND ACCESSORIES:

- Watercolor markers
- Crayons
- Grease pencil
- Damp cloth/sponge

VARIATIONS AND EXTENSIONS:

1. Prepare a second chart without the broken lines for the numeral and word.
2. If developmentally appropriate, extend the sets of ties beyond the number six.

WHAT'S FOR LUNCH?

DEVELOPMENTAL GOALS:

1. To recognize letters of the alphabet
2. To associate an object with the printed word
3. To identify foods that can be served for lunch
4. To communicate through the written word

RELATED CURRICULUM THEMES:

Foods

Occupations

Senses

Fruits/Vegetables

Community Helpers

Restaurants

My Body

Cooking

Health

DIRECTIONS:

1. On a sheet of tagboard, use a felt-tip marker to print the title What's for lunch?
2. Divide the remainder of the piece of tagboard into six squares, using a ruler and felt-tip marker.
3. In each square, draw or cut and paste pictures of six nutritional foods that can be served for lunch.
4. Cut from a piece of manuscript paper strips to place under each square.
5. Glue the manuscript paper under each object.
6. On the top line of each piece of paper, print the name of the object.
7. Cover the chart with clear Con-Tact paper or laminate it.

TOOLS AND ACCESSORIES:

- Watercolor markers
- Crayons
- Grease pencil

VARIATIONS AND EXTENSIONS:

1. The children could copy the word that has been printed directly below it.
2. Additional charts could be made depicting breakfast or dinner foods.

CHAPTER 7

ANIMAL AND INSECT CARDS

dpecker

dpecker

geese

owls

DEVELOPMENTAL GOALS:

1. To associate the printed name with an animal or insect

2. To develop an appreciation for the printed word

3. To develop visual discrimination skills

4. To develop problem-solving skills

5. To develop eye–hand coordination skills

6. To practice forming letters

7. To develop small-muscle coordination skills

RELATED CURRICULUM THEMES:

Bugs	Letters	Animal Families
Insects and Spiders	Pets	Zoo Animals
Farm Animals	Wild Animals	Water Animals
Communication	Nature	Sounds

DIRECTIONS:

1. Collect an assortment of animal and insect pictures from magazines and calendars.
2. Use rubber cement or glue to mount the pictures on sheets of colored construction paper. (*See photograph.*)
3. Draw lines, or glue a strip of manuscript paper, under each picture.
4. Print the name of the animal or insect on the top line.
5. Using broken lines, print the name of the animal or insect again.
6. Cover each sheet with clear Con-Tact paper or laminate it.

TOOLS AND ACCESSORIES:

- Watercolor markers
- Crayons
- Grease pencil
- Damp cloth/sponge

VARIATIONS AND EXTENSIONS:

1. This activity could be adapted to a variety of themes.
2. If developmentally appropriate, omit the name of the animal or insect.

LEARNING ABOUT DOGS

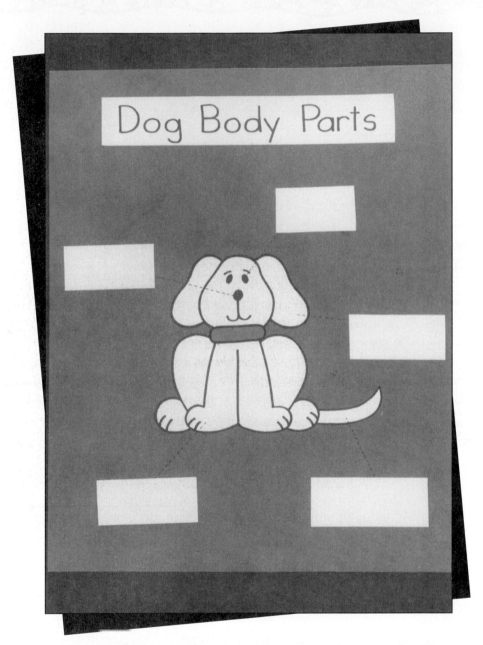

Dog Body Parts

DEVELOPMENTAL GOALS:

1. To identify in writing the body parts of a dog
2. To develop an appreciation for the printed word
3. To develop visual discrimination skills
4. To develop problem-solving skills
5. To develop eye–hand coordination skills
6. To develop small-muscle coordination skills

RELATED CURRICULUM THEMES:

Dogs	Pets	Animals
Friends	Reading	Writing

DIRECTIONS:

1. Select a bright red piece of tagboard.
2. Draw a dog on a piece of white construction paper. (*See photograph.*)
3. Use a black felt-tip marker to outline the dog and to add eyes, nose, mouth, and paws. Color the collar red using CRAY-PAS or a felt-tip marker. Place the dog in the center of the tagboard sheet and glue it.
4. Cut or make a seventeen-inch strip of manuscript paper. Print the title Dog Body Parts on it. Glue to top of tagboard sheet.
5. Cut five strips five inches each in length. Glue a strip near the dog's eyes, nose, mouth, paws, and tail.
6. Cover the chart with clear Con-Tact paper or laminate it.

TOOLS AND ACCESSORIES:

- Watercolor markers
- Crayons
- Grease pencil
- Damp cloth/sponge

VARIATIONS AND EXTENSIONS:

This chart can be adapted to other animals.

I CAN WRITE WORDS

I can write words.

curling iron	glove	tree
leaf	computer	comb
cake	car	lamp
telephone	snowperson	crayon

DEVELOPMENTAL GOALS:

1. To practice writing the names of objects
2. To develop an appreciation for the printed word
3. To develop visual discrimination skills
4. To develop problem-solving skills
5. To develop eye–hand coordination skills
6. To practice forming letters
7. To develop small-muscle coordination skills

RELATED CURRICULUM THEMES:

Words

My World

Symbols

Color

Communication

Writing Tools

DIRECTIONS:

1. Across the top of a piece of tagboard, print the title I can write words.
2. Draw a horizontal line below the title across the tagboard piece.
3. Divide the remainder of the tagboard into twelve squares. (*See photograph*.)
4. Draw an object in each of the twelve squares.
5. Use felt-tip markers to add color to each of the objects.
6. Add detail and outline each object using a felt-tip marker.
7. Print the name of the object under it in each box.
8. Cover the finished piece with clear Con-Tact paper or laminate it.

TOOLS AND ACCESSORIES:

- Watercolor markers
- Crayons
- Grease pencil
- Damp cloth/sponge

VARIATIONS AND EXTENSIONS:

1. Create additional charts using names related to the curriculum themes.
2. If developmentally appropriate, omit the first letter of the object.

MODES OF TRANSPORTATION

DEVELOPMENTAL GOALS:

1. To associate the words for different modes of transportation
2. To practice correct letter formation
3. To practice small muscle coordination skills
4. To communicate in writing
5. To develop an appreciation for the printed word
6. To develop eye–hand coordination skills

RELATED CURRICULUM THEMES:

Vehicles	Transportation	Machines
Occupations	Safety	Shapes
Wheels	Water	Signs
Travel	Letters	Directions

DIRECTIONS:

1. Draw or trace an airplane, train, car, boat, and truck on construction paper.
2. Cut out each of the figures.
3. Use a felt-tip marker to add details. (*See photograph*.)
4. Print, using broken lines, the name of each object on it.
5. Cover the pieces with clear Con-Tact paper or laminate them.

TOOLS AND ACCESSORIES:

- Watercolor markers
- Crayons
- Grease pencil
- Damp cloth/sponge

VARIATIONS AND EXTENSIONS:

1. Relate this activity to other themes. Examples include buildings, animals, clothing, safety, signs, foods, tools, and furniture.
2. The children can trace and cut their own shapes.

NOUNS

Nouns

Read each sentence. Draw a circle around the right noun.

1. The _____ is cold.
   (ice cream, Ann, sun)

2. _____ run fast.
   (Turtles, Horses, Snails)

3. _____ grow to become dogs.
   (Fish, Puppies, Kittens)

4. _____ can fly.
   (Birds, Fish, Puppies)

5. _____ can bark.
   (Cats, Turtles, Dogs)

6. _____ lay eggs.
   (Dogs, Hens, Pigs)

7. _____ like to play.
   (Books, Cats, Trees)

DEVELOPMENTAL GOALS:

1. To practice selecting nouns to complete a sentence
2. To develop an appreciation for the printed word
3. To develop visual discrimination skills
4. To develop problem-solving skills
5. To develop eye–hand coordination skills
6. To develop small-muscle coordination skills

RELATED CURRICULUM THEMES:

The Alphabet

Writing Tools

Writing

Nouns

Communication

Symbols

DIRECTIONS:

1. Print and center the title Nouns across the top of a large piece of lined manuscript chart paper. (*See photograph.*)
2. Under the title, print the directions: Read each sentence. Draw a circle around the right noun.
3. Leave a blank line. Then print the following:
   a. The _____ is cold. (Ice cream, Ann, or Sun)
   b. _____ run fast. (Turtles, Horses, or Snails)
   c. _____ grow to become dogs. (Fish, Puppies, or Kittens)
   d. _____ can fly. (Birds, Fish, or Puppies)
   e. _____ can bark. (Cats, Turtles, or Dogs)
   f. _____ lay eggs. (Dogs, Hens, or Pigs)
   g. _____ like to play. (Books, Cats, or Trees)
4. Cover the finished piece with clear Con-Tact paper or laminate it.

TOOLS AND ACCESSORIES:

- Watercolor markers
- Crayons
- Grease pencil
- Damp cloth/sponge

VARIATIONS AND EXTENSIONS:

1. Provide materials for children to make noun books.
2. Create additional charts using *nouns*.
3. Design a bulletin board that includes the caption Nouns. Encourage the children to cut out magazine pictures and label. Post the pictures on the bulletin board.

MORE NOUNS

More Nouns

Read each sentence. Draw a circle around the right noun.

1. _____ drive on the road.
   (Airplanes, Cars, Dogs)
2. _____ live in water.
   (Horses, Pigs, Fish)
3. _____ live in houses.
   (People, Fish, Snakes)
4. _____ make nests.
   (Pigs, Birds, Sheep)
5. _____ are small.
   (Horses, Ants, Elephants)
6. _____ make people laugh.
   (Cakes, Clowns, Coats)
7. _____ are to read.
   (Bats, Boats, Books)

DEVELOPMENTAL GOALS:

1. To practice selecting nouns to complete a sentence
2. To develop an appreciation for the printed word
3. To develop visual discrimination skills
4. To develop problem-solving skills
5. To develop eye–hand coordination skills
6. To develop small-muscle coordination skills
7. To practice forming letters

RELATED CURRICULUM THEMES:

Sentences

Writing Tools

Writing

Nouns

Communication

Symbols

DIRECTIONS:

1. Print and center the title More Nouns across the top of a large piece of lined manuscript chart paper. (*See photograph*.)
2. Under the title, print the directions: Read each sentence. Draw a circle around the right noun.
3. Leave a blank line. Then print the following:
    a. _____ drive on the road. (Airplanes, Cars, or Dogs)
    b. _____ live in the water. (Horses, Pigs, or Fish)
    c. _____ live in houses. (People, Fish, or Snakes)
    d. _____ make nests. (Pigs, Birds, or Sheep)
    e. _____ are small. (Horses, Ants, or Elephants)
    f. _____ make people laugh. (Cakes, Clowns, or Coats)
    g. _____ are to read. (Bats, Boats, Books)
4. Cover the finished piece with clear Con-Tact paper or laminate it.

TOOLS AND ACCESSORIES:

- Watercolor markers
- Crayons
- Grease pencil
- Damp cloth/sponge

VARIATIONS AND EXTENSIONS:

This chart can be varied by providing a clue for the children. Print the first letter of the noun in the blank provided.

OBJECTS

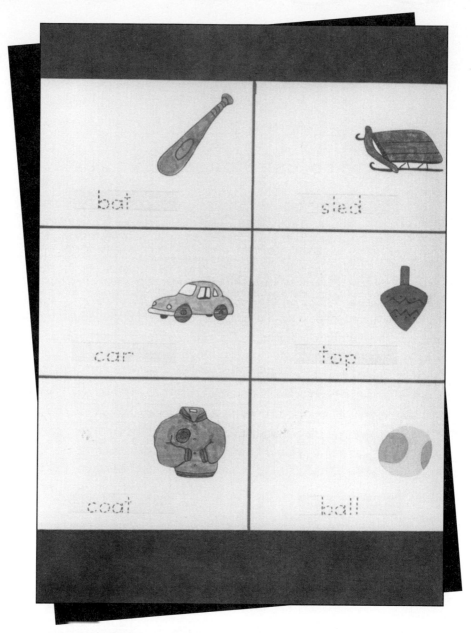

bat

sled

car

top

coat

ball

DEVELOPMENTAL GOALS:

1. To associate the printed word with an object
2. To develop an appreciation for the printed word
3. To develop visual discrimination skills
4. To develop eye–hand coordination skills
5. To practice forming letters
6. To develop small-muscle coordination skills

RELATED CURRICULUM THEMES:

My World
The Alphabet

Printing
Communication

Writing
Words

DIRECTIONS:

1. Use a ruler and marker to divide a piece of tagboard into six boxes. (*See photograph.*)
2. Draw or paste the picture of an object in each box.
3. Attach a strip of manuscript paper or draw lines in each box.
4. Print, using broken lines, the name of each object on the lines.
5. Cover the finished piece with clear Con-Tact paper or laminate it.

TOOLS AND ACCESSORIES:

- Watercolor markers
- Crayons
- Grease pencil
- Damp cloth/sponge

VARIATIONS AND EXTENSIONS:

1. Substitute other objects related to a theme or to the children's interests.
2. Omit the names of the objects. Instead, encourage the children to print them on the space provided, using a set of name cards for reference.

SELECTING NOUNS

Selecting Nouns

Read each sentence. Write the correct word on the line.

1. The _____ is hot.
   (sun - fun)

2. The _____ is cold.
   (rice - ice)

3. The _____ can roll.
   (ball - call)

4. The _____ is new.
   (moat - coat)

5. The _____ has a hole.
   (pail - bail)

6. The _____ is furry.
   (fat - cat)

DEVELOPMENTAL GOALS:

1. To practice forming alphabet letters
2. To practice selecting nouns to complete a sentence
3. To develop an appreciation for the printed word
4. To develop visual discrimination skills
5. To develop problem-solving skills
6. To develop eye–hand coordination skills
7. To develop small-muscle coordination skills

RELATED CURRICULUM THEMES:

Symbols

Writing Tools

Writing

Writing Surfaces

Communication

Alphabet

DIRECTIONS:

1. Print and center the title Selecting Nouns across the top of lined manuscript chart paper. (*See photograph.*)
2. Under the title, print the directions: Read each sentence. Write the correct word on the line.
3. Leave a blank line. Then print the following:
   a. The _____ is hot. (sun or fun)
   b. The _____ is cold. (rice or ice)
   c. The _____ can roll. (ball or call)
   d. The _____ is new. (moat or coat)
   e. The _____ has a hole. (pail or bail)
   f. The _____ is furry. (fat or cat)
4. Cover the finished piece with clear Con-Tact paper or laminate it.

TOOLS AND ACCESSORIES:

- Watercolor markers
- Crayons
- Grease pencil
- Damp cloth/sponge

VARIATIONS AND EXTENSIONS:

Create charts that use other nouns.

SELECTING MORE NOUNS

Selecting More Nouns
Read each sentence. Write
the correct word on the line.

1. The _____ runs.
   (log-dog)
2. The _____ hides.
   (kitten-mitten)
3. The _____ is large.
   (tall-ball)
4. The _____ reads books.
   (can-man)
5. The _____ broke.
   (toy-joy)
6. The _____ is black.
   (sat-hat)

DEVELOPMENTAL GOALS:

1. To practice selecting nouns to complete a sentence
2. To develop an appreciation for the printed word
3. To develop visual discrimination skills
4. To develop problem-solving skills
5. To develop eye–hand coordination skills
6. To develop small-muscle coordination skills
7. To practice forming letters

RELATED CURRICULUM THEMES:

Reading

Writing Tools

Writing

Symbols

Communication

Nouns

DIRECTIONS:

1. Print and center the title Selecting More Nouns across the top of lined manuscript chart paper. (*See photograph.*)
2. Under the title, print the directions: Read each sentence. Write the correct word on the line.
3. Leave a blank line. Then print the following:
   a. The _____ runs. (log or dog)
   b. The _____ hides. (kitten or mitten)
   c. The _____ is large. (tall or ball)
   d. The _____ reads books. (can or man)
   e. The _____ broke. (toy or joy)
   f. The _____ is black. (sat or hat)
4. Cover the finished piece with clear Con-Tact paper or laminate it.

TOOLS AND ACCESSORIES:

- Watercolor markers
- Crayons
- Grease pencil
- Damp cloth/sponge

VARIATIONS AND EXTENSIONS:

1. Create charts using other nouns.
2. Make a bulletin board titled Nouns. You or the children can prepare pictures of objects to attach to the board. Word cards for the pictures could be prepared and placed near the corresponding picture.

THINGS IN MY WORLD

DEVELOPMENTAL GOALS:

1. To practice correct letter formation
2. To communicate in writing
3. To develop an appreciation for the printed word
4. To practice small-muscle coordination skills

RELATED CURRICULUM THEMES:

Toys

Vehicles

Colors

Sports

Shapes

Seasons

DIRECTIONS:

1. Draw various objects on tagboard.
2. Cut out each item.
3. Add detail to the objects with felt-tip markers or CRAY-PAS.
4. Cut out strips of manuscript paper and paste one onto each item. (*See photograph.*)
5. Print, using broken lines, the name of each item on the manuscript strip.
6. Cover the finished pieces with clear Con-Tact paper or laminate them.

TOOLS AND ACCESSORIES:

- Watercolor markers
- Crayons
- Grease pencil
- Damp cloth/sponge

VARIATIONS AND EXTENSIONS:

The children could prepare word cards to match the objects.

TOOL DICTIONARY

rake • novel • Tool Dictionary • crew • clamp • nail • liers • hoe • hammer • brush • file

DEVELOPMENTAL GOALS:

1. To identify the names of different tools
2. To practice forming letters
3. To develop problem-solving skills
4. To communicate in writing
5. To develop eye–hand coordination skills
6. To develop an appreciation for the printed word

RELATED CURRICULUM THEMES:

Construction Tools

Homes

Families

Communication

Occupations

Sounds

Buildings

Hobbies

Safety

DIRECTIONS:

1. Cut eight-by-eight-inch squares of tagboard.
2. Print the title Tool Dictionary on a piece of tagboard to be used as a cover.
3. Trace a picture of a different tool on each of the remaining pieces of tagboard. (*See photograph.*)
4. Color each tool using crayons or felt-tip markers.
5. Print the names of the tools across the bottom of the tagboard pieces.
6. Cover the finished pieces with clear Con-Tact paper or laminate them.

TOOLS AND ACCESSORIES:

- Pencils
- Paper
- Watercolor markers

VARIATIONS AND EXTENSIONS:

1. The children can read this book and identify each item by picture and/or word.
2. On a separate sheet of paper, the children can copy the words from the book.

TOOL LOTTO

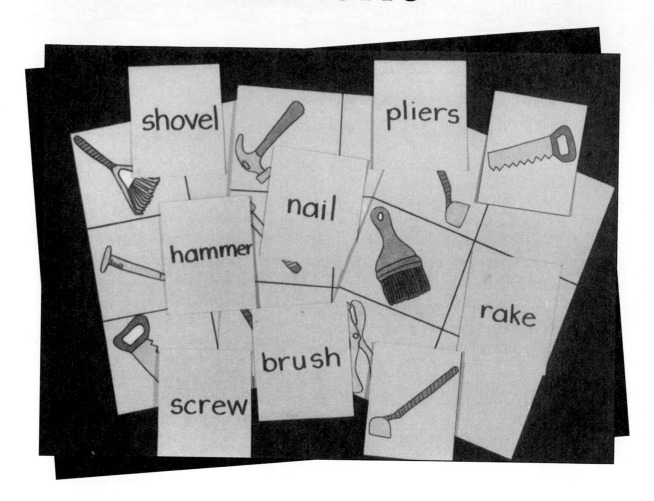

DEVELOPMENTAL GOALS:

1. To associate an object with the printed word
2. To communicate in writing
3. To develop an appreciation for the printed word
4. To develop eye–hand coordination
5. To practice taking turns

RELATED CURRICULUM THEMES:

Community Helpers

Homes

Hobbies

Construction Tools

Safety

Communication

Occupations

Families

Buildings

DIRECTIONS:

1. Cut a large piece of tagboard into two fifteen-by-fifteen-inch pieces. (*See photograph.*)
2. Divide the two pieces into six five-inch squares, using a medium felt-tip marker.
3. Cut one of the tagboard pieces into six squares.
4. Draw a different tool on each of the six squares.
5. Draw an identical tool in each of the squares on the larger tagboard piece.
6. Cover the chart with clear Con-Tact paper or laminate.

TOOLS AND ACCESSORIES:

- Paper or tagboard
- Crayons
- Pencils
- Stickers

VARIATIONS AND EXTENSIONS:

1. Provide paper and tagboard for the children to construct their own games.
2. Stickers can be provided to make additional games.

WORDS-I-KNOW SET

Bb blocks	Cc coat	Jj jack
Rr robe	Words I know	Ss shorts
Ss skirt	Tt top	Tt truck

DEVELOPMENTAL GOALS:

1. To develop an appreciation for the printed word
2. To develop problem-solving skills
3. To develop eye–hand coordination skills
4. To associate the written word with an object
5. To practice the correct formation of letters
6. To communicate in writing

RELATED CURRICULUM THEMES:

Things in My World	Toys	Clothes
Animals	Our Town	Vehicles
Signs	Holidays	Flowers
People	Family	Sports

DIRECTIONS:

1. Cut seven-by-ten-inch pieces of cardboard.
2. Print the title Words I Know on one of the pieces of cardboard.
3. Draw a sketch or cut and paste pictures of objects on the remaining pieces.
4. Print the name of the object under each picture.
5. Print the upper and lowercase alphabet beginning letter.
6. Cover pieces with clear Con-Tact paper or laminate.

TOOLS AND ACCESSORIES:

- Pencils
- Paper

VARIATIONS AND EXTENSIONS:

1. Encourage the children to record words that they know. Make a book of the words they know by stapling sheets of paper together.
2. Prepare a book of familiar objects, and place it in the writing center.

WRITING TOOLS

Writing Tools

crayon

chalk

pencil

pen

marker

DEVELOPMENTAL GOALS:

1. To associate writing tools with their printed names
2. To develop small muscle coordination skills
3. To practice forming letters
4. To develop visual discrimination skills
5. To communicate using a writing tool

RELATED CURRICULUM THEMES:

Art

Letters

Communication

Writing Tools

We Create

Symbols

DIRECTIONS:

1. Print the title Writing Tools across the top of a piece of tagboard. (*See photograph.*)
2. Draw a piece of chalk, a crayon, a marker, a pen, and a pencil in a column down the left side of the tagboard.
3. Use a soft-leaded pencil to lightly print in a broken line format for the name of each object.
4. Trace over the names of the objects with a felt-tip marker. If needed, also outline objects with the felt-tip marker. To add interest, color can also be added.
5. Cover the chart with clear Con-Tact paper or laminate it.

TOOLS AND ACCESSORIES:

- Watercolor markers
- Crayons
- Damp cloth/sponge

VARIATIONS AND EXTENSIONS:

The chart could contain eating utensils or construction tools.

CHAPTER 8

FISH WORD PUZZLE • PUZZLES • WHAT IS IN THE PICTURE?

FISH WORD PUZZLE

Fish Word Puzzle

Look at the words on the fish. Find them in the puzzle. Circle the words.

fish   me
dish   see
wish   bee

f i s h m
b t d s e
e w i s h
e p s e e
n e h o p

DEVELOPMENTAL GOALS:

1. To find the printed words in the puzzle
2. To develop an appreciation for the printed word
3. To develop visual discrimination skills
4. To develop problem-solving skills
5. To develop eye–hand coordination skills
6. To practice forming letters
7. To develop small-muscle coordination skills

RELATED CURRICULUM THEMES:

Alphabet	Matching	Communication
Symbols	Reading	Puzzles

DIRECTIONS:

1. Across the top of a piece of tagboard, print the title Fish Word Puzzle. (*See photograph.*)
2. Under that, print these directions: Look at the words on the fish. Find them in the puzzle. Circle the words.
3. Cut a fish from orange construction paper and glue it on the tagboard.
4. Print these words on the fish:
   - fish
   - dish
   - wish
   - me
   - see
   - bee
5. Under the fish, print the following letter sequence:

f	i	s	h	m
b	t	d	s	e
e	w	i	s	h
e	p	s	e	e
n	e	h	o	p

6. Cover the finished piece with clear Con-Tact paper or laminate it.

TOOLS AND ACCESSORIES:

- Watercolor markers
- Crayons
- Grease pencil
- Damp cloth/sponge

VARIATIONS AND EXTENSIONS:

This teaching aid could be adapted to almost any curriculum theme.

PUZZLES

Puzzles
Look at the picture. Fill in the missing letters.

1. _ _ t
2. _ l _ _ _ _
3. r _ _ _ _
4. _ _ k _

rake   cake   plant   ant

DEVELOPMENTAL GOALS:

1. To identify the missing letters
2. To develop an appreciation for the printed word
3. To develop visual discrimination skills
4. To develop problem-solving skills
5. To develop eye–hand coordination skills
6. To practice forming letters
7. To develop small-muscle coordination skills

RELATED CURRICULUM THEMES:

Alphabet	Writings	Communication
Symbols	Reading	Our World

DIRECTIONS:

1. Across the top of a piece of tagboard, print the title Puzzles. (*See photograph.*)
2. Under that, print the directions:

   Look at the picture. Fill in the missing letters.
3. On a piece of manuscript paper, print the numeral 1. Next to it, draw two short lines. Then print the letter *t*.
4. Print the numeral 2. Next to it, draw a short line, followed by the letter *l*, and three additional short lines.
5. Print the numeral 3. Next to it, print an *r*. Then draw three short lines.
6. Print the numeral 4. Next to it, draw two short lines. Then print the letter *k*, followed by another short line.
7. Across the bottom of the chart, draw a rake, a cake, a plant, and an ant. Under each item, print its name.
8. To create appeal, add color to the items pictured.
9. Cover the chart with clear Con-Tact paper or laminate it.

TOOLS AND ACCESSORIES:

- Watercolor markers
- Crayons
- Grease pencil
- Damp cloth/sponge

VARIATIONS AND EXTENSIONS:

This puzzle can be adapted to any curriculum theme.

WHAT IS IN THE PICTURE?

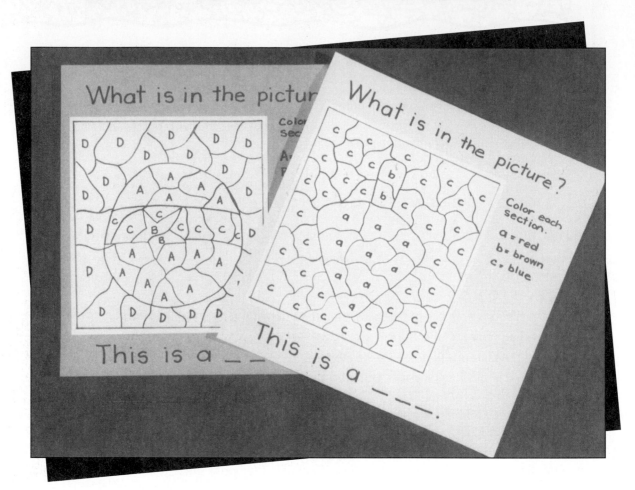

DEVELOPMENTAL GOALS:

1. To develop eye–hand coordination skills

2. To identify letters of the alphabet

3. To develop an appreciation for the printed word

4. To practice problem-solving and prediction skills

RELATED CURRICULUM THEMES:

Things in My World

Writing Tools

Colors

The Alphabet

Writing

Pictures

DIRECTIONS:

1. Choose a piece of colored construction paper that is 13 1/2-X-18 inches.

2. Paste an 8 1/2-X-11-inch piece of paper on the construction paper. (*See photograph*.)

3. Draw a border on an 8 1/2-X-11-inch piece of paper to form a frame. Above the frame print, "What is in the picture?"

4. Draw a simple object—such as a ball, hat, or top—inside the frame.

5. Divide the object into smaller segments with lines. Print a letter, to represent a color, in each section. (*See photograph*.)

6. Record a code for coloring each section, such as:

   A = blue   B = yellow   C = red   D = black

7. At the bottom of the construction paper, print, "This is a" and then draw short lines for each letter in the word.

8. Cover the finished piece with clear Con-Tact paper or laminate it.

TOOLS AND ACCESSORIES:

- Watercolor markers
- Crayons
- Damp cloth/sponge

VARIATIONS AND EXTENSIONS:

1. Encourage the children to make their own picture puzzles.

2. Print the name of the object on the back of the puzzle.

C H A P T E R   9

ALPHABETIZE THE NAMES • CORRECT WORDS • DRAW A . . . • DRAW A PICTURE • DRAWING • DIFFERENCES • DRAW A SHAPE • MORE DIFFERENCES • MY FAMILY • NAME A PET • OPPOSITES • SIX BOXES • STICKER MATCHING CARDS • TRACING PATTERN CARDS • WHICH WORD IS RIGHT?

ALPHABETIZE THE NAMES

Alphabetize the names.	
Tasha	
Frank	
Patrick	
Russell	
Christopher	
Morgan	
Joey	
Alyssa	
Luke	
Justin	
Kathy	
Lindsay	
Matt	
Richie	
Jessica	

DEVELOPMENTAL GOALS:

1. To practice placing names in alphabetical order
2. To develop an appreciation for the printed word
3. To develop visual discrimination skills
4. To develop problem-solving skills
5. To develop eye–hand coordination skills
6. To practice forming letters
7. To develop small-muscle coordination skills

RELATED CURRICULUM THEMES:

Alphabet Letters   Communication   Names
Our School   Friends   Writing

DIRECTIONS:

1. Across the top of a piece of tagboard, print the title Alphabetize the names.
2. Draw a horizontal line under the title.
3. Divide the remaining tagboard in half by making a vertical line down the middle. (*See photograph*.)
4. Print, in random order, the names of the children in your classroom.
5. Cover the finished piece with clear Con-Tact paper or laminate it.

TOOLS AND ACCESSORIES:

- Watercolor markers
- Crayons
- Grease pencil
- Damp cloth/sponge

VARIATIONS AND EXTENSIONS:

1. Make a chart to alphabetize vocabulary words associated with curriculum themes.
2. Make a chart to alphabetize holiday words.

CORRECT WORDS

Correct Words

Look at the picture and words. Cross out the letter that does not belong.

trukck

hate

kaite

pendcil

rapbbit

botok

ttree

DEVELOPMENTAL GOALS:

1. To identify the letter that does not belong in a word
2. To develop an appreciation for the printed word
3. To develop visual discrimination skills
4. To develop problem-solving skills
5. To develop eye–hand coordination skills
6. To develop small-muscle coordination skills

RELATED CURRICULUM THEMES:

Our Alphabet

Reading

Symbols

Our World

Communication

Writing

DIRECTIONS:

1. Across the top of a piece of tagboard, print the title Correct Words.
2. Under the title, print these directions: Look at the picture and words. Cross out the letter that does not belong.
3. Draw a truck. Next to it, print "trukck." (*See photograph.*)
4. Draw a hat. Next to it, print "hate."
5. Draw a kite. Next to it, print "kaite."
6. Draw a pencil. Next to it, print "pendcil."
7. Draw a rabbit. Next to it, print "rapbbit."
8. Draw a book. Next to it, print "botok."
9. Draw a tree. Next to it, print "ttree."
10. Create visual appeal by adding color to the objects.
11. Cover the finished piece with clear Con-Tact paper or laminate it.

TOOLS AND ACCESSORIES:

- Watercolor markers
- Crayons
- Grease pencil
- Damp cloth/sponge

VARIATIONS AND EXTENSIONS:

This teaching aid could be adapted to almost any curriculum theme.

DRAW A . . .

DEVELOPMENTAL GOALS:

1. To identify farm animal words
2. To draw three farm animals: a cow, a horse, and a pig
3. To develop an appreciation for the printed word
4. To develop visual discrimination skills
5. To develop problem-solving skills
6. To develop eye–hand coordination skills
7. To develop small-muscle coordination skills

RELATED CURRICULUM THEMES:

Farm Animals

Safety

Games

Farms

Pets

Words

DIRECTIONS:

1. Glue brown construction paper over the lower section of a piece of tagboard. (*See photograph.*)
2. Glue light-blue construction paper over the remaining tagboard.
3. Sketch and cut out clouds and a fence from white construction paper.
4. Sketch and cut out a sun from yellow construction paper.
5. Sketch and cut out a barn from red construction paper.
6. Glue or paste the clouds, fence, sun, and barn onto the tagboard.
7. Print the title Draw a . . . on the tagboard.
8. Print the word "cow" on the lower left side, "horse" in the middle, and "pig" on the right side of the tagboard sheet.
9. Cover the chart with clear Con-Tact paper or laminate it.

TOOLS AND ACCESSORIES:

- Watercolor markers
- Crayons
- Grease pencil
- Damp cloth/sponge

VARIATIONS AND EXTENSIONS:

1. This concept could be adapted to a variety of themes, such as zoo animals, house pets, birds, fish, and pond animals.

DRAW A PICTURE

Draw a picture.
Read each sentence. Then
draw a picture for the
sentences.

1. The pink flower has green
   leaves.

2. The tree has yellow apples.

3. The man has a red truck.

DEVELOPMENTAL GOALS:

1. To practice drawing a picture
2. To develop an appreciation for the printed word
3. To develop visual discrimination skills
4. To develop problem-solving skills
5. To develop eye–hand coordination skills
6. To practice forming letters
7. To develop small-muscle coordination skills

RELATED CURRICULUM THEMES:

Symbols

Writing Tools

Writing

Our Alphabet

Communication

Art

DIRECTIONS:

1. Center the title Draw a picture across the top of lined manuscript chart paper. (*See photograph*.)
2. Under the title, print these directions: Read each sentence. Then draw a picture for the sentences.
3. Leave a blank line under the directions. Then print the following sentences, leaving two blank lines between each to give the children space to draw:

    a. The pink flower has green leaves.

    b. The tree has yellow apples.

    c. The man has a red truck.

6. Cover the finished piece with clear Con-Tact paper or laminate it.

TOOLS AND ACCESSORIES:

- Watercolor markers
- Crayons
- Grease pencil
- Damp cloth/sponge

VARIATIONS AND EXTENSIONS:

1. Adapt the chart to the classroom curriculum theme.
2. Encourage the children to develop their own charts by providing materials in the writing center.

DRAWING

Draw a picture.
Read the sentences.
Follow the directions.
1. Draw a tree.
2. Put seven apples on it.
3. Color two apples green.
4. Color five apples red.

DEVELOPMENTAL GOALS:

1. To practice following written directions
2. To develop an appreciation for the printed word
3. To develop visual discrimination skills
4. To develop problem-solving skills
5. To develop eye–hand coordination skills
6. To develop small-muscle coordination skills

RELATED CURRICULUM THEMES:

The Alphabet

Creativity

Art

Reading

Communication

Directions

DIRECTIONS:

1. Select a colored piece of tagboard.
2. Cut a piece of lined paper that is eight lines long and is one and a half inches smaller than the tagboard in width. (*See photograph*.)
3. Center the title Draw a picture on the first line.
4. On the remaining lines print: Read the sentences. Follow the directions:
   a. Draw a tree.
   b. Put seven apples on it.
   c. Color two apples green.
   d. Color five apples red.
5. Center and paste the piece of lined paper on the tagboard.
6. Cut a fourteen-by-ten-inch piece of white construction paper.
7. Paste it three-quarters of an inch below the lined paper.
8. Cover the finished piece with clear Con-Tact paper or laminate it.

TOOLS AND ACCESSORIES:

- Watercolor markers
- Crayons
- Grease pencil
- Damp cloth/sponge

VARIATIONS AND EXTENSIONS:

This teaching aid can be adapted to most curriculum themes. Use the same format, but change the directions.

DIFFERENCES

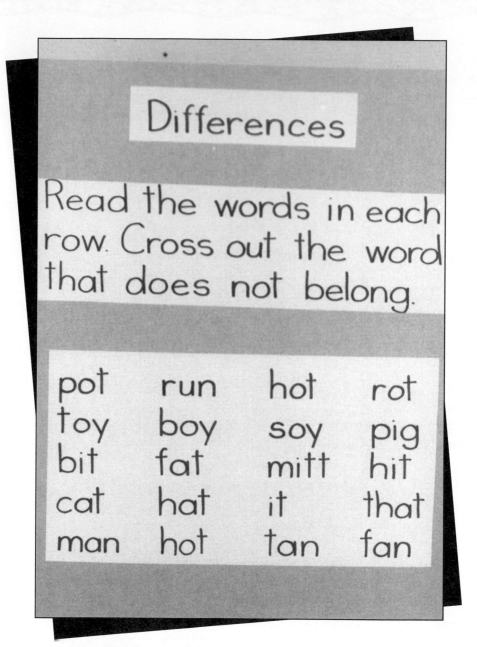

Differences

Read the words in each row. Cross out the word that does not belong.

pot	run	hot	rot
toy	boy	soy	pig
bit	fat	mitt	hit
cat	hat	it	that
man	hot	tan	fan

DEVELOPMENTAL GOALS:

1. To practice following written directions
2. To identify words that are different
3. To develop an appreciation for the printed word
4. To develop visual discrimination skills
5. To develop problem-solving skills
6. To develop eye–hand coordination skills
7. To develop small-muscle coordination skills

RELATED CURRICULUM THEMES:

Differences   Reading   Communication

DIRECTIONS:

1. Choose a large piece of colored tagboard.
2. Cut from a piece of lined paper the following: A single line for the title. Three lines for the directions. A piece with five lines for the words
3. Print the title Differences on the single line of paper. Center and paste or glue this strip on the tagboard. (*See photograph.*)
4. Print the following on the triple strip: Read the words in each row. Cross out the word that does not belong.
5. Paste the directions three inches under the title.
6. Print on the remaining piece of lined paper the following:

pot	run	hot	rot
toy	boy	soy	pig
bit	fat	mitt	hit
cat	hat	it	that
man	hot	tan	fan

7. Paste this piece three inches under the directions.
8. Cover the finished piece with clear Con-Tact paper or laminate it.

TOOLS AND ACCESSORIES:

- Watercolor markers
- Crayons
- Grease pencil
- Damp cloth/sponge

VARIATIONS AND EXTENSIONS:

1. Prepare a similar chart for opposites.
2. If developmentally appropriate, charts representing other word families can be prepared and introduced.

DRAW A SHAPE

Draw a shape.

circle	square
rectangle	triangle
diamond	oval

DEVELOPMENTAL GOALS:

1. To identify basic shapes
2. To develop eye–hand coordination skills
3. To associate the printed word with its symbol
4. To practice forming letters

RELATED CURRICULUM THEMES:

Letters
Communicating

Words
Our World

Shapes
Writing

DIRECTIONS:

1. Print the title Draw a Shape across the top of a piece of tagboard.
2. Divide the remainder of the tagboard into six equal boxes. (*See photograph.*)
3. In each box, print, using broken lines, the name of one shape: circle, square, rectangle, triangle, diamond, and oval.
4. Cover the finished piece with clear Con-Tact paper or laminate it.

TOOLS AND ACCESSORIES:

- Watercolor markers
- Crayons
- Grease pencil
- Damp cloth/sponge
- Corresponding laminated shapes

VARIATIONS AND EXTENSIONS:

1. Make a chart titled Draw a toy or Draw a vehicle.
2. Provide materials for the children to make a chart. Across the top of the paper, print Draw a . . . Provide a line for them to decide what will be drawn.

MORE DIFFERENCES

More Differences
Read the words in each
row. Cross out the word
that does not belong.

ball	bat	doll	shirt
pants	cup	tie	belt
dog	bus	bird	cat
chair	table	bed	coat
spoon	cup	glue	plate
red	rat	yellow	blue
bus	car	bee	truck
shoe	square	circle	triangle

DEVELOPMENTAL GOALS:

1. To follow written directions
2. To select the word that does not belong in a series
3. To develop an appreciation for the printed word
4. To develop visual discrimination skills
5. To develop problem-solving skills
6. To develop eye–hand coordination skills
7. To develop small-muscle coordination skills

RELATED CURRICULUM THEMES:

Differences   Reading   Communication

DIRECTIONS:

1. Center the title More Differences across the top of lined manuscript chart paper. (*See photograph.*)
2. Under the title print these directions: Read the words in each row. Cross out the word that does not belong.
3. Leave a blank line. Then print the following:

ball	bat	doll	shirt
pants	cup	tie	belt
dog	bus	bird	cat
chair	table	bed	coat
spoon	cup	glue	plate
red	rat	yellow	blue
bus	car	bee	truck
shoe	square	circle	triangle

4. Cover the finished piece with clear Con-Tact paper or laminate it.

TOOLS AND ACCESSORIES:

- Watercolor markers
- Crayons
- Grease pencil
- Damp cloth/sponge

VARIATIONS AND EXTENSIONS:

Adapt the chart to the current classroom curriculum theme.

MY FAMILY

My family

I have ___ people
in my family.
Their names are

_____

_____.

DEVELOPMENTAL GOALS:

1. To visually represent family members
2. To print the names of family members
3. To record a numeral representing the members of one's family
4. To practice communicating in writing
5. To develop eye–hand coordination skills

RELATED CURRICULUM THEMES:

Families

Numerals

Alphabet Letters

Communication

Names

Drawing

Brothers and Sisters

Writing Tools

Art

DIRECTIONS:

1. Draw a horizontal line across the midline of a large piece of tagboard.
2. Cut the piece of tagboard in half.
3. Turn the tagboard vertically. (*See photograph.*)
4. Print the title My Family at the top.
5. Draw a picture frame on the tagboard.
6. Color in the frame, using a brown felt-tip marker.
7. If desired, add detail by outlining the frame and adding corner angles and distress marks.
8. Print the following under the frame:

   I have _____ people in my family.

   Their names are _____

   _____

9. Cover the finished piece with clear Con-Tact paper or laminate.

TOOLS AND ACCESSORIES:

- Watercolor markers
- Damp cloth/sponge

VARIATIONS AND EXTENSIONS:

1. This material could be adapted to other themes, such as My Friends, My Toys, and My Favorite Person.
2. Each day, a different child could share his family picture and talk about his family.
3. Using construction paper, make a chart for each child. When completed, post the charts in the classroom.

NAME A PET

Name a pet.
Think of a name for each pet
Write it on the line.

DEVELOPMENTAL GOALS:

1. To follow written directions
2. To identify and write the name of a pet on the line provided
3. To develop an appreciation for the printed word
4. To develop visual discrimination skills
5. To develop problem-solving skills
6. To develop eye–hand coordination skills
7. To develop small-muscle coordination skills
8. To practice forming letters and numerals

RELATED CURRICULUM THEMES:

Pets

Writing Tools

Writing

Names

Communication

Our Alphabet

DIRECTIONS:

1. Cut or make a piece of lined chart paper. (*See photograph.*)
2. Center the title Name a Pet at the top of the paper.
3. Leave a space, then print: Think of a name for each pet. Print it on the line.
4. Down the left side of the paper, draw a cat, dog, fish, and rabbit.
5. To add interest, use colored markers to highlight the pets.
6. Cover the finished piece with clear Con-Tact paper or laminate it.

TOOLS AND ACCESSORIES:

- Watercolor markers
- Crayons
- Grease pencil
- Damp cloth/sponge

VARIATIONS AND EXTENSIONS:

1. This teaching aid could be adapted to include objects related to most curriculum themes.
2. If developmentally appropriate, the project could be changed to one of the following:

   Name a tree

   Name a bird

   Name a vehicle

   Name the clothing

   Name the food

   Name the toy

   Name the tool

3. Encourage the children to develop their own charts.

OPPOSITES

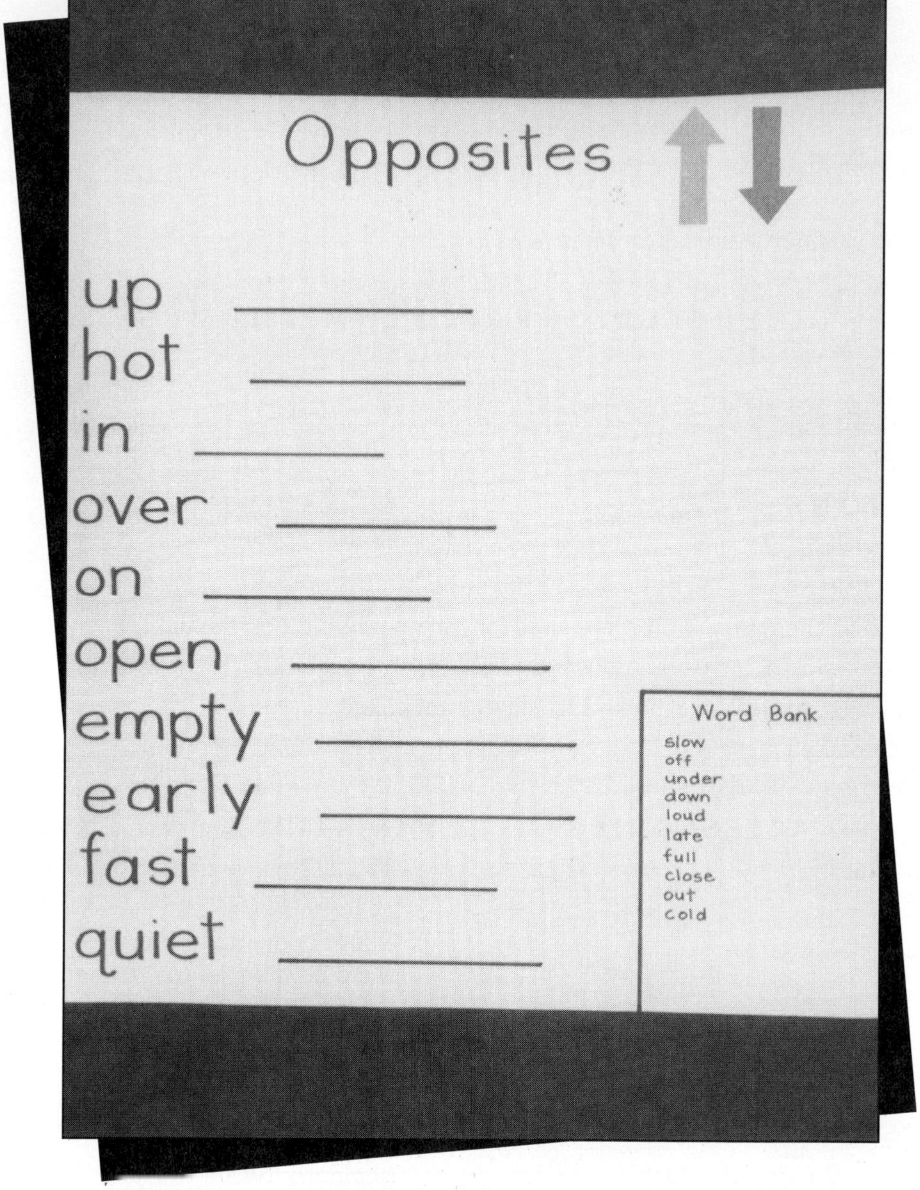

Opposites

up _____

hot _____

in _____

over _____

on _____

open _____

empty _____

early _____

fast _____

quiet _____

Word Bank
slow
off
under
down
loud
late
full
close
out
cold

DEVELOPMENTAL GOALS:

1. To develop the concept of opposite word meanings
2. To develop an appreciation for the printed word
3. To develop visual discrimination skills
4. To develop problem-solving skills
5. To develop eye–hand coordination skills
6. To practice forming letters
7. To develop small-muscle coordination skills

RELATED CURRICULUM THEMES:

Words

Alphabet Letters

Opposites

Writing

Communication

DIRECTIONS:

1. Print the title Opposites across the top of a piece of tagboard.
2. Down the left side of the tagboard, print these words:
   - up
   - on
   - hot
   - open
   - in
   - empty
   - over
   - early
   - fast
   - quiet

   (*See photograph.*)
3. In the lower right corner of the tagboard, draw an eight-by-seven-inch box.
4. Print the title Word Bank at the top of the box.
5. Down the left side of the box, print these words:
   - slow
   - loud
   - off
   - late
   - under
   - full
   - down
   - close
   - out
   - cold
6. Cover the finished piece with clear Con-Tact paper or laminate it.

TOOLS AND ACCESSORIES:
- Watercolor markers
- Crayons
- Grease pencil
- Damp cloth/sponge

VARIATIONS AND EXTENSIONS:
A chart could be made using other words that are opposite in meaning.

SIX BOXES

Six Boxes

1. In the first box, draw a ball.
2. In the second box, draw a tree.
3. In the third box, draw a house.
4. In the fourth box, draw a car.
5. In the fifth box, draw a dog.
6. In the sixth box, write your name.

DEVELOPMENTAL GOALS:

1. To practice reading and following directions
2. To develop an appreciation for the printed word
3. To develop visual discrimination skills
4. To develop problem-solving skills
5. To develop eye–hand coordination skills
6. To develop small-muscle coordination skills
7. To practice forming letters and numerals

RELATED CURRICULUM THEMES:

Our Alphabet

Drawing

Writing Tools

Directions

Communication

Reading

DIRECTIONS:

1. Choose a large piece of colored tagboard.
2. Cut or make a piece of thirteen-by-twenty-two-inch manuscript paper.
3. Using a black felt-tip marker, print the following on the writing paper:

   Six Boxes
   a. In the first box, draw a ball.
   b. In the second box, draw a tree.
   c. In the third box, draw a house.
   d. In the fourth box, draw a car.
   e. In the fifth box, draw a dog.
   f. In the sixth box, write your name.
4. Paste the directions on the piece of tagboard.
5. Cut six pieces of white paper, 3 1/2 x 5 inches each. Print a numeral on each in the upper left corner, beginning with 1 and ending with 6.
6. Paste the six pieces of paper across the lower section of the tagboard.
7. Cover the finished piece with clear Con-Tact paper or laminate it.

TOOLS AND ACCESSORIES:

- Watercolor markers
- Crayons
- Grease pencil
- Damp cloth/sponge

VARIATIONS AND EXTENSIONS:

The objects can be changed to reflect the children's environment or the curriculum theme.

STICKER MATCHING CARDS

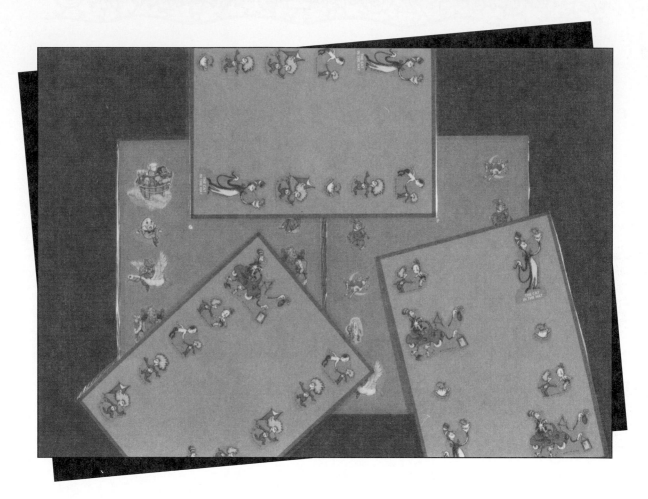

DEVELOPMENTAL GOALS:

1. To develop visual discrimination skills
2. To develop problem-solving skills
3. To develop eye–hand coordination skills
4. To develop small-muscle coordination skills

RELATED CURRICULUM THEMES:

Matching   Objects   Our World

Likenesses   Differences   Sticker Fun

DIRECTIONS:

1. Cut a piece of large tagboard into twelve-by-fifteen-inch pieces.
2. Paste a vertical column of individual stickers on the left side of the tagboard pieces.
3. Paste identical stickers along the rightside of tagboard, changing the order.
4. Cover the cards with clear Con-Tact paper or laminate them.

TOOLS AND ACCESSORIES:

- Watercolor markers
- Crayons
- Grease pencil
- Damp cloth/sponge

VARIATIONS AND EXTENSIONS:

1. During the holidays, use stickers that reflect the season.
2. Encourage the children to make their own sticker matching boards.

TRACING PATTERN CARDS

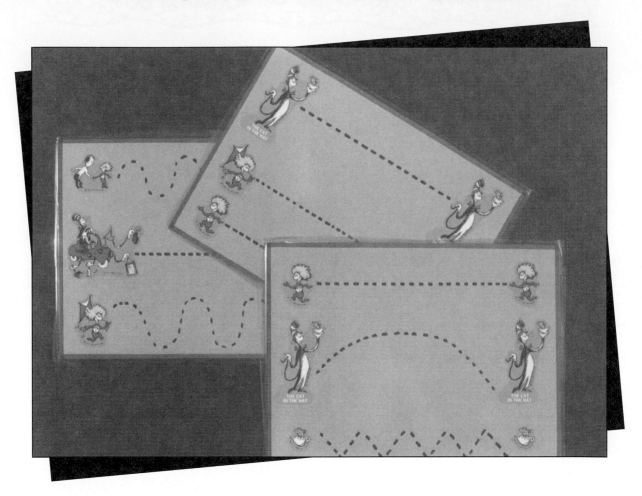

DEVELOPMENTAL GOALS:

1. To develop eye–hand coordination skills
2. To develop small-muscle coordination skills
3. To develop visual discrimination skills
4. To develop problem-solving skills

RELATED CURRICULUM THEMES:

Writing   Communication   Our World

DIRECTIONS:

1. Select colored tagboard and cut into twelve-by-fourteen-inch pieces.
2. Purchase stickers from a school supply store or draw objects for the left and right margins of tagboard pieces. (*See photograph.*)
3. If objects are drawn, add color to create interest.
4. Draw various broken-line patterns (straight line, wavy line, zig-zag line, etc.) between the objects on the right and left margins.
5. Use a felt-tip marker to draw a border around the tagboard, if desired.
6. Cover the pieces with clear Con-Tact paper or laminate them.

TOOLS AND ACCESSORIES:

- Watercolor markers
- Crayons
- Grease pencil
- Damp cloth/sponge

VARIATIONS AND EXTENSIONS:

1. If developmentally appropriate, create more difficult patterns.
2. Cards reflecting holiday themes can be developed. Examples include: pumpkins for Halloween, flags for the Fourth of July, turkeys for Thanksgiving, trees for Christmas, hearts for Valentine's Day, and eggs and baskets for Easter.
3. Cards can also be adapted for curriculum themes, such as animals, vehicles, tools, foods, baskets, pets, and breads.

WHICH WORD IS RIGHT?

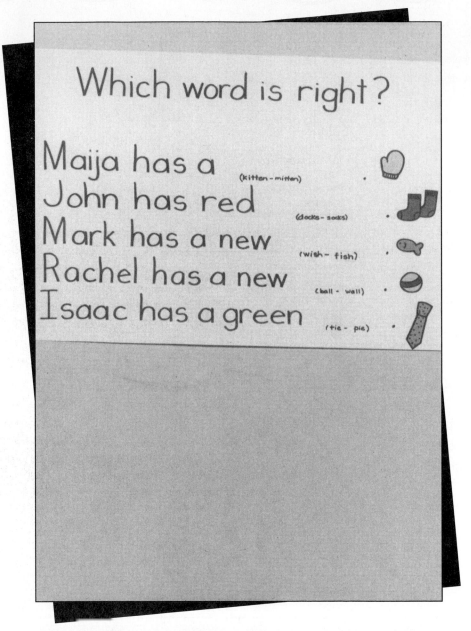

Which word is right?

Maija has a _____ (kitten - mitten)

John has red _____ (clocks - socks)

Mark has a new _____ (wish - fish)

Rachel has a new _____ (ball - wall)

Isaac has a green _____ (tie - pie)

DEVELOPMENTAL GOALS:

1. To practice decoding the written word
2. To develop an appreciation for the printed word
3. To develop visual discrimination skills
4. To develop problem-solving skills
5. To develop eye–hand coordination skills
6. To develop small-muscle coordination skills
7. To practice forming letters

RELATED CURRICULUM THEMES:

Our Alphabet

Rhyming Words

Reading

Word Families

Communication

Directions

DIRECTIONS:

1. Cut or make a piece of lined manuscript chart paper.
2. Across the top of the paper, print the title Which word is right?
3. Leave one blank line.
4. Print the numeral 1. Next to it, print "Maija has a" and leave a space. Make a period and draw a mitten. Under the space, print the words "kitten" and "mitten" and enclose them in parentheses. (See *photograph*.)
5. Print the numeral 2. Next to it, print "John has a red" and leave a space. Make a period and draw a sock. Under the space, print the words "docks" and "socks" and enclose them in parentheses.
6. Print the numeral 3. Next to it, print "Mark has a new" and leave a space. Make a period and draw a fish. Under the space, print the words "wish" and "fish" and enclose them in parentheses.
7. Print the numeral 4. Next to it, print "Rachel has a new" and leave a space. Make a period and draw a ball. Under the space, print the words "ball" and "wall" and enclose them in parentheses.
8. Print the numeral 5. Next to it, print "Isaac has a green" and leave a space. Make a period and draw a tie. Under the space, print the words "tie" and "pie" and enclose them in parentheses.
9. To create interest, add color to the objects.
10. Cover the finished piece with clear Con-Tact paper or laminate it.

TOOLS AND ACCESSORIES:

- Watercolor markers
- Crayons
- Grease pencil
- Damp cloth/sponge

VARIATIONS AND EXTENSIONS:

1. This teaching aid could be adapted to the vocabulary related to almost any theme.
2. Use the same format, but change the names to those of the children in your class.

ALL ABOUT DOGS

All About Dogs

A dog has ____ legs.

A dog has ____ tail.

A dog drinks _____.

A dog can wag its ____.

A dog can ____.

Word Bank
bark
one
water
two
tail

DEVELOPMENTAL GOALS:

1. To read an incomplete sentence and fill in the appropriate word from a word bank
2. To develop an appreciation for the printed word
3. To develop visual discrimination skills
4. To develop problem-solving skills
5. To develop eye–hand coordination skills
6. To practice forming letters
7. To develop small-muscle coordination skills

RELATED CURRICULUM THEMES:

Dogs

Friends

Pets

Reading

Animals

Writing

DIRECTIONS:

1. At the top of a sheet of tagboard, center the title All About Dogs.
2. On the tagboard, print the following: (*See photograph.*)

   A dog has _____ legs.

   A dog drinks _____.

   A dog can _____.

   A dog has _____ tail.

   A dog can wag its _____.

3. Draw a six-by-nine-inch box centered at the bottom of the tagboard.
4. In the box, print the title WORD BANK.
5. Down the left side of the box, print these words: bark, one, water, four, tail.
6. Cover the finished piece with clear Con-Tact paper or laminate it.

TOOLS AND ACCESSORIES:

- Watercolor markers
- Crayons
- Grease pencil
- Damp cloth/sponge

VARIATIONS AND EXTENSIONS:

1. This chart can be adapted to any curriculum theme.
2. Additional sentences could be added to the chart.

CREATING SENTENCES

Creating Sentences

Sentences are statements. A sentence must make sense. Draw a line to the best ending.

Dogs   cry.
Birds   bark.
Babies   chirp.
Jets   swim.
Turtles   fly.
Fish   crawl.

DEVELOPMENTAL GOALS:

1. To identify a sentence as a statement
2. To create sentences by combining words
3. To develop an appreciation for the printed word
4. To develop visual discrimination skills
5. To develop problem-solving skills
6. To develop eye–hand coordination skills
7. To develop small-muscle coordination skills

RELATED CURRICULUM THEMES:

Creating Sentences
Our Alphabet
Writing Tools

Reading
Writing
Symbols

Our World
Communication
Books

DIRECTIONS:

1. Cut or make a piece of lined chart paper.
2. Across the top of the paper, print the title Creating Sentences.
3. Leave a blank line.
4. Print the following: Sentences are statements. A sentence must make sense. Draw a line to the best ending.
5. Leave another blank line, then, down the left side, print these words: dogs, birds, babies, jets, turtles, and fish. (*See photograph.*)
6. Down the right side, print these words: cry, bark, chirp, swim, fly, and crawl.
7. To provide the children an example of a sentence, draw a line from the word "dogs" to the word "bark."
8. Cover the finished piece with clear Con-Tact paper or laminate it.

TOOLS AND ACCESSORIES:

- Watercolor markers
- Crayons
- Grease pencil
- Damp cloth/sponge

VARIATIONS AND EXTENSIONS:

1. This teaching aid can be adapted to most themes.
2. Use the same format, but change the verbs.

CREATING MORE SENTENCES

Creating More Sentences

Sentences are statements. A sentence must make sense. Draw a line to the best ending.

Matt and Eric   is swimming.
The pony   are brothers
The fish   are purring.
The rabbits   is new.
The cats   are hopping.
My jump rope   is running.

DEVELOPMENTAL GOALS:

1. To learn that a sentence is a statement
2. To create sentences by combining words
3. To develop an appreciation for the printed word
4. To develop visual discrimination skills
5. To develop problem-solving skills
6. To develop eye–hand coordination skills
7. To develop small-muscle coordination skills

RELATED CURRICULUM THEMES:

Reading
Creating Sentences
Writing Tools

Writing
Our World
Symbols

Communication
Our Alphabet

DIRECTIONS:

1. Cut or make a piece of lined chart paper.
2. Across the top of the paper, print the title Creating More Sentences.
3. Leave a blank line.
4. Print the following: Sentences are statements. A sentence must make sense. Draw a line to the best ending.
5. Leave another blank line, then, down the left side of the paper, print the following: Matt and Eric, The pony, The fish, The rabbits, The cats, My jump rope.
6. Across from these phrases, print the following: is swimming, are brothers, are purring, is new, are hopping, is running.
7. To provide the children an example of a sentence, draw a line from "Matt and Eric" to the words "are brothers." (*See photograph.*)
8. Cover the finished piece with clear Con-Tact paper or laminate it.

TOOLS AND ACCESSORIES:

- Watercolor markers
- Crayons
- Grease pencil
- Damp cloth/sponge

VARIATIONS AND EXTENSIONS:

1. This teaching aid can be adapted to most curriculum themes.
2. Use the same format, but change the sentence endings.
3. Substitute the names of children in your class.

A DOG STORY

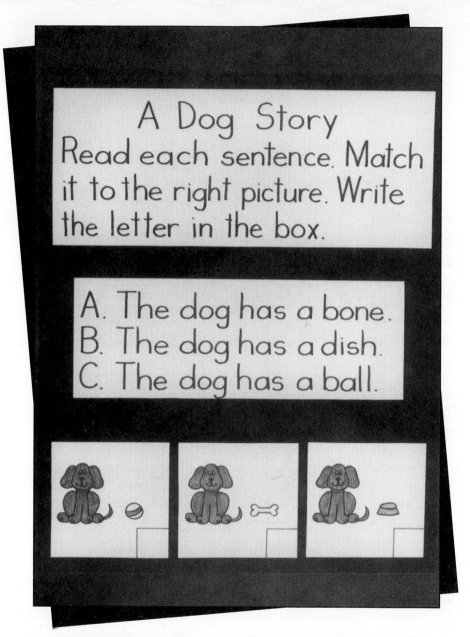

A Dog Story
Read each sentence. Match
it to the right picture. Write
the letter in the box.

A. The dog has a bone.
B. The dog has a dish.
C. The dog has a ball.

DEVELOPMENTAL GOALS:

1. To match a sentence to a corresponding picture
2. To develop an appreciation for the printed word
3. To develop visual discrimination skills
4. To develop problem-solving skills
5. To develop eye–hand coordination skills
6. To practice forming letters
7. To develop small-muscle coordination skills

RELATED CURRICULUM THEMES:

Sentences	Our World	Writing
Reading	Words	Symbols
Communication	Dogs	Pets

DIRECTIONS:

1. Across the top of a piece of heavy manuscript paper, print the title A Dog Story.
2. Under the title, print these directions: Read each sentence. Match it to the right picture. Write the letter in the box.
3. Under that, print the options:
   A. The dog has a bone.
   B. The dog has a dish.
   C. The dog has a ball.
4. Cut the directions and options from the paper. Glue them on a sheet of tagboard. (*See photograph.*)
5. Draw three dogs on 5" x 5" squares of construction paper. In the first square draw a dog with a ball. In the second square, draw a dog with a bone. In the third square, draw a dog with a bowl.
6. Add color to the drawings and paste them across the bottom of the tagboard.
7. Cover the finished piece with clear Con-Tact paper or laminate it.

TOOLS AND ACCESSORIES:

- Watercolor markers
- Crayons
- Grease pencil
- Damp cloth/sponge

VARIATIONS AND EXTENSIONS:

1. Develop a story related to the curriculum theme.
2. Additional sentences and corresponding pictures could be added to the chart.

"IS" AND "ARE"

"Is" and "Are"
Read each line. Choose a helping word to finish the sentence. Write the word.

1. The dog _____ sleeping.
    (is · are)

2. The dogs _____ sleeping.
    (is · are)

3. Susy _____ running.
    (is · are)

4. Susy and Ty _____ running.
    (is · are)

5. He _____ going to school.
    (is · are)

6. They _____ going to school.
    (is · are)

DEVELOPMENTAL GOALS:

1. To practice selecting the correct verb form to complete a sentence
2. To develop an appreciation for the printed word
3. To develop visual discrimination skills
4. To develop problem-solving skills
5. To develop eye–hand coordination skills
6. To develop small-muscle coordination skills
7. To practice forming letters

RELATED CURRICULUM THEMES:

The Alphabet

Writing Tools

Writing

Speech

Communication

Literature

DIRECTIONS:

1. Center the title Is and Are at the top of a large piece of lined manuscript chart paper. (*See photograph*.)
2. Under the title, print these directions: Read each line. Choose a helping word to finish the sentence. Write the word.
3. Leave a blank line. Then print the following:

   1. The dog _____ sleeping. (is–are)
   2. The dogs _____ sleeping. (is–are)
   3. Suzy _____ running. (is–are)
   4. Suzy and Ty _____ running. (is–are)
   5. He _____ going to school. (is–are)
   6. They _____ going to school. (is–are)

4. Cover the finished piece with clear Con-Tact paper or laminate it.

TOOLS AND ACCESSORIES:

- Watercolor markers
- Crayons
- Grease pencil
- Damp cloth/sponge

VARIATIONS AND EXTENSIONS:

1. Use the names of children from your class in the sentences.

MAKE A SENTENCE

Make a sentence.
Draw a circle around the
word to make a sentence.

1. The man has a (hat - sat).
2. The lady likes her (cat - pat)
3. The boy has a (fat - bat).
4. The dog was (fat - hat).
5. The shoes are on a (pat - mat).
6. It looked like a (rat - pat).

DEVELOPMENTAL GOALS:

1. To practice forming sentences
2. To develop an appreciation for the printed word
3. To develop visual discrimination skills
4. To develop problem-solving skills
5. To develop eye–hand coordination skills
6. To develop small-muscle coordination skills

RELATED CURRICULUM THEMES:

Our Alphabet
Symbols

Writing Surfaces
Writing

Communication
Writing Tools

DIRECTIONS:

1. Print the title Make a sentence across the top of a large piece of lined manuscript chart paper. (*See photograph*.)
2. Under the title, print the directions: Draw a circle around the word to make a sentence.
3. Leave a blank line. Then print the following:

   a. The man has a (hat–sat).

   b. The lady likes her (cat–pat).

   c. The boy has a (fat–bat).

   d. The dog was (fat–hat).

   e. The shoes are on a (pat–mat).

   f. It looked like a (rat–pat).

4. Cover the finished piece with clear Con-Tact paper or laminate it.

TOOLS AND ACCESSORIES:

- Watercolor markers
- Crayons
- Grease pencil
- Damp cloth/sponge

VARIATIONS AND EXTENSIONS:

Create charts using such word families as *an* and *it*.

MAKE A QUESTION

Make a question.
Draw a line to make a question.

1. Where are   run away?
2. Does Luis   school start?
3. What is   my shoes?
4. When will   wear glasses?
5. Where is   her name?
6. Will the dog   the ball?

DEVELOPMENTAL GOALS:

1. To make a question by drawing a line between two sets of words
2. To develop an appreciation for the printed word
3. To develop visual discrimination skills
4. To develop problem-solving skills
5. To develop eye–hand coordination skills
6. To develop small-muscle coordination skills

RELATED CURRICULUM THEMES:

Questions

Our World

Reading

Our Alphabet

Communication

Symbols

DIRECTIONS:

1. Cut or make a piece of lined chart paper.
2. At the top of the paper center the title Make a question.
3. Leave one blank line.
4. Print the numeral 1. Next to it, print "Where are" and leave a space. Then print the words "run away," followed by a question mark.
5. Print the numeral 2. Next to it, print "Does Luis" and leave a space. Then print the words "school start," followed by a question mark.
6. Print the numeral 3. Next to it, print "What is" and leave a space. Then print the words "my shoes," followed by a question mark.
7. Print the numeral 4. Next to it, print "When will" and leave a space. Then print the words "wear glasses," followed by a question mark.
8. Print the numeral 5. Next to it, print "Where is" and leave a space. Then print the words "her name," followed by a question mark.
9. Print the numeral 6. Next to it, print "Will the dog" and leave a space. Then print the words "the ball," followed by a question mark.
10. To provide the children an example, draw a broken line from "Where are" to "my shoes?"
11. Cover the finished piece with clear Con-Tact paper or laminate it.

TOOLS AND ACCESSORIES:

- Watercolor markers
- Crayons
- Grease pencil
- Damp cloth/sponge

VARIATIONS AND EXTENSIONS:

1. This teaching aid could be adapted to the vocabulary of almost any curriculum theme.
2. Use the same format, but change the names to those of the children in your class.

MORE "IS" AND "ARE"

More "Is" and "Are"

Read each line. Choose a helping word to finish the sentence. Write the word.

1. The boys _____ fishing.
   (is · are)
2. The boy _____ fishing.
   (is · are)
3. The cat _____ purring.
   (is · are)
4. The cats _____ purring.
   (is · are)
5. The horses _____ running.
   (is · are)
6. The horse _____ running.
   (is · are)

DEVELOPMENTAL GOALS:

1. To learn the correct verb form needed to complete a sentence
2. To develop an appreciation for the printed word
3. To develop visual discrimination skills
4. To develop problem-solving skills
5. To develop eye–hand coordination skills
6. To develop small-muscle coordination skills
7. To practice forming letters

RELATED CURRICULUM THEMES:

The Alphabet

Writing Tools

Writing

Speech

Communication

Literature

DIRECTIONS:

1. Print the title More Is and Are across the top of a large piece of lined manuscript chart paper. (*See photograph.*)
2. Under the title, print these directions: Read each line. Choose a helping word to finish the sentence. Write the word.
3. Leave a blank line. Then print the following:

   1. The boys _____ fishing. (is–are)
   2. The boy _____ fishing. (is–are)
   3. The cat _____ purring. (is–are)
   4. The cats _____ purring. (is–are)
   5. The horses _____ running. (is–are)
   6. The horse _____ running. (is–are)

4. Cover the finished piece with clear Con-Tact paper or laminate it.

TOOLS AND ACCESSORIES:

- Watercolor markers
- Crayons
- Grease pencil
- Damp cloth/sponge

VARIATIONS AND EXTENSIONS:

Create additional charts using the names of children from your class.

MORE SENTENCES

More Sentences

Read each question. Change the question. Make it a statement.

Can Kim write?

1.

Will Ting play?

2.

Will Mother come?

3.

Can Jeff wash the dishes?

4.

Can Sylvia jump?

5.

Will Stevie dance?

6.

DEVELOPMENTAL GOALS:

1. To practice writing sentences
2. To develop an appreciation for the printed word
3. To develop visual discrimination skills
4. To develop problem-solving skills
5. To develop eye–hand coordination skills
6. To develop small-muscle coordination skills
7. To understand the difference between statements and questions

RELATED CURRICULUM THEMES:

Our Alphabet

Symbols

Writing Tools

Writing

Communication

Books

DIRECTIONS:

1. Center the title More Sentences at the top of a large piece of lined manuscript chart paper. (*See photograph.*)
2. Under the title, print these directions: Read each question. Change the question. Make it a statement.
3. Leave a blank line.
4. Print, using small letters, the following:
   a. Can Kim write?
   b. Will Ting play?
   c. Will Mother come?
   d. Can Jeff wash the dishes?
   e. Can Sylvia jump?
   f. Will Steve dance?
5. Cover the finished piece with clear Con-Tact paper or laminate it.

TOOLS AND ACCESSORIES:

- Watercolor markers
- Crayons
- Grease pencil
- Damp cloth/sponge

VARIATIONS AND EXTENSIONS:

1. Use the names of children in your class in the sentences.
2. Adapt the sentences to the curriculum theme.

MORE SENTENCE SENSE

More Sentence Sense
Read the words. Write a sentence that makes sense.

1. yellow sun is The

2. apple is The red

3. purple The are grapes

4. grow Flowers seeds from

5. trees Oranges on grow

6. the Potatoes grow ground in

DEVELOPMENTAL GOALS:

1. To practice writing sentences that make sense
2. To develop an appreciation for the printed word
3. To develop visual discrimination skills
4. To develop problem-solving skills
5. To develop eye–hand coordination skills
6. To develop small-muscle coordination skills
7. To practice forming letters

RELATED CURRICULUM THEMES:

Our World

Stories

Writing Tools

Writing

Communication

Sentences

DIRECTIONS:

1. Print the title More Sentence Sense across the top of a large piece of lined manuscript chart paper. (*See photograph.*)
2. Under the title, print these directions: Read the words. Write a sentence that makes sense.
3. Leave a blank line. Then print the following:

   yellow sun is The

   apple is The red

   purple The are grapes

   grow Flowers seeds from

   trees Oranges on grow

   the Potatoes grow ground in

4. Cover the finished piece with clear Con-Tact paper or laminate it.

TOOLS AND ACCESSORIES:

- Watercolor markers
- Crayons
- Grease pencil
- Damp cloth/sponge

VARIATIONS AND EXTENSIONS:

Use words that reflect the curriculum theme.

ONE WORD TOO MANY

One Word Too Many

Write the word that completes the sentence.

1. Close the _____. (floor - door)
2. The egg is in the _____. (pan - fan)
3. Jack drove the _____. (far - car)
4. Alecia ate with a _____. (moon - spoon)
5. The apple had a _____. (reed - seed)
6. The pen is _____. (pack - black)
7. The dog has a _____. (tail - pail)
8. A kitten grows to be a _____. (bat - cat)

DEVELOPMENTAL GOALS:

1. To write words that complete the sentence
2. To develop an appreciation for the printed word
3. To develop visual discrimination skills
4. To develop problem-solving skills
5. To develop eye–hand coordination skills
6. To practice forming letters
7. To develop small-muscle coordination skills

RELATED CURRICULUM THEMES:

Sentences	Communication	Words
Reading	Writing	Our World
Symbols	Rhymes	Word Families

DIRECTIONS:

1. Across the top of a piece of heavy manuscript paper, print the title One Word Too Many.
2. Under the title, print the following: Write the word that completes the sentence.

   Close the _____ (floor–door).

   The egg is in the _____ (pan–tan).

   Jack drove the _____ (tar–car).

   Alecia ate with a _____ (moon–spoon).

   The apple had a _____ (reed–seed).

   The pen is _____ (pack–black).

   The dog has a _____ (tail–pail).

   The kitten grows to be a _____ (bat–cat).

3. Cover the finished piece with clear Con-Tact paper or laminate.

TOOLS AND ACCESSORIES:

- Watercolor markers
- Crayons
- Grease pencil
- Damp cloth/sponge

VARIATIONS AND EXTENSIONS:

1. Develop sentences related to the curriculum theme.
2. If developmentally appropriate, construct longer sentences.

QUESTIONS

? ? ? ? ? ? Questions ? ? ? ? ?
Read each sentence. Write
a new sentence to ask a
question.

Claude can cook.
1. Can Claude cook?

Kris will ski.
2.

Kelsi can skip.
3.

Wendy can dance.
4.

Della is acting.
5.

Derek will help the cat.
6.

DEVELOPMENTAL GOALS:

1. To practice writing questions
2. To develop an appreciation for the printed word
3. To develop visual discrimination skills
4. To develop problem-solving skills
5. To develop eye–hand coordination skills
6. To develop small-muscle coordination skills
7. To practice forming letters

RELATED CURRICULUM THEMES:

Questions

The Alphabet

Writing Tools

Reading

Communication

Symbols

DIRECTIONS:

1. Center the title Questions at the top of a large piece of lined chart paper.
2. Use a colored felt-tip pen to make question marks on each side of the title. (*See photograph.*)
3. Under the title, print these directions: Read each sentence. Write a new sentence to ask a question.
4. Print, using small letters, "Claude can cook." Under it, write the question, "Can Claude cook?" to provide an example.
5. Continue by printing the following:

   Kris will ski.

   Kelsi can skip.

   Wendy can dance.

   Della is acting.

   Derek will help the cat.

6. Cover the finished piece with clear Con-Tact paper or laminate it.

TOOLS AND ACCESSORIES:

- Watercolor markers
- Crayons
- Grease pencil
- Damp cloth/sponge

VARIATIONS AND EXTENSIONS:

1. Use the names of children in your class in the sentences.
2. Use other verbs, such as hop, ride, cook, paint, sing, draw, write, swim, read, and jump.
3. Adapt chart to a curriculum theme.

MORE QUESTIONS

? ? ? More Questions ? ? ? ? ?
? ?
Read each sentence. Write
a new sentence to ask a
question.

Fido can bark.

1.

Jo-Anne is swimming.

2.

Luke will sing.

3.

Karen is running.

4.

Carlos can play football.

5.

Peter will help Anna.

6.

DEVELOPMENTAL GOALS:

1. To practice writing questions
2. To develop an appreciation for the printed word
3. To develop visual discrimination skills
4. To develop problem-solving skills
5. To develop eye–hand coordination skills
6. To develop small-muscle coordination skills
7. To practice forming letters

RELATED CURRICULUM THEMES:

Questions

The Alphabet

Reading

Writing Tools

Communication

Symbols

DIRECTIONS:

1. Center the title More Questions at the top of a large piece of lined chart paper.
2. Use a colored felt-tip pen to make question marks on each side of the title. (*See photograph.*)
3. Under the title, print these directions: Read each sentence. Write a new sentence to ask a question.
4. Print, using small letters, the following:

   Fido can bark.

   Jo-Anne is swimming.

   Luke will sing.

   Karen is running.

   Carlos can play football.

   Peter will help Anna.

   Cover the finished piece with clear Con-Tact paper or laminate it.

TOOLS AND ACCESSORIES:

- Watercolor markers
- Crayons
- Grease pencil
- Damp cloth/sponge

VARIATIONS AND EXTENSIONS:

1. Use the names of children in your class in the sentences.
2. Rewrite the chart using other verbs.
3. Encourage the children to create charts.

SEE, SAW, AND SEEN

"See," "Saw" and "Seen"
Read each line. Choose the correct word to complete the sentence.

1. Antonio _____ a clown.
   (see, saw, seen)

2. He had _____ the clown before.
   (see, saw, seen)

3. I _____ an elephant yesterday.
   (see, saw, seen)

4. Pam _____ a monkey.
   (see, saw, seen)

5. She had not _____ one before.
   (see, saw, seen)

6. Robert _____ one this morning.
   (see, saw, seen)

DEVELOPMENTAL GOALS:

1. To choose the correct verb tense for a sentence
2. To develop an appreciation for the printed word
3. To develop visual discrimination skills
4. To develop problem-solving skills
5. To develop eye–hand coordination skills
6. To develop small-muscle coordination skills
7. To practice forming letters

RELATED CURRICULUM THEMES:

Our Speech   Writing   Communication
Writing Tools   Sentences   Reading

DIRECTIONS:

1. Center the title See, Saw, and Seen at the top of a large piece of lined chart paper. (*See photograph.*)
2. Under the title, print these directions: Read each line. Choose the correct word to complete the sentence.
3. Leave a blank line. Then print the following:

   1. Antonio _____ a clown. (see, saw, seen)
   2. He had _____ the clown before. (see, saw, seen)
   3. I _____ an elephant yesterday. (see, saw, seen)
   4. Pam _____ a monkey. (see, saw, seen)
   5. She had not _____ one before. (see, saw, seen)
   6. Robert _____ one this morning. (see, saw, seen)

4. Cover the finished piece with clear Con-Tact paper or laminate it.

TOOLS AND ACCESSORIES:

- Watercolor markers
- Crayons
- Grease pencil
- Damp cloth/sponge

VARIATIONS AND EXTENSIONS:

This chart can be designed to provide the children with a clue. Place an *e*, an *a*, or an *n* in the correct place on the blank line.

SENTENCES

Sentences

Read each question. Change the question. Make it a statement.

Will Olivia eat?
1. Olivia will eat.

Is Candy playing?
2.

Will Marla sleep?
3.

Can Victor sing?
4.

Is Patrick happy?
5.

Can Carole read?
6.

DEVELOPMENTAL GOALS:

1. To practice writing sentences
2. To understand the difference between statements and questions
3. To develop an appreciation for the printed word
4. To develop visual discrimination skills
5. To develop problem-solving skills
6. To develop eye–hand coordination skills
7. To develop small-muscle coordination skills
8. To practice forming letters

RELATED CURRICULUM THEMES:

Our Alphabet

Symbols

Writing Tools

Writing

Communication

Reading

DIRECTIONS:

1. Center the title Sentences at the top of a large piece of manuscript chart paper. (*See photograph.*)
2. Under the title, print these directions: Read each question. Change the question. Make it a statement.
3. Leave a blank line.
4. Print, using small letters, Will Olivia eat? Provide an example of a statement by printing, Olivia will eat.
5. Print the remaining questions, using small letters:
   a. Is Candy playing?
   b. Will Marla sleep?
   c. Can Victor sing?
   d. Is Patrick happy?
   e. Can Carole read?
6. Cover the finished piece with clear Con-Tact paper or laminate it.

TOOLS AND ACCESSORIES:

- Watercolor markers
- Crayons
- Grease pencil
- Damp cloth/sponge

VARIATIONS AND EXTENSIONS:

1. Use the names of children in your class in the sentences.
2. Adapt the sentences to the curriculum theme.

SENTENCE SENSE

Sentence Sense
Read the words. Write a
sentence that makes sense

1. cake I like

2. fun Dogs are

3. David cakes bakes

4. play Kittens to like

5. fort a Aaron made

6. cereal ate Lindsay

DEVELOPMENTAL GOALS:

1. To practice writing sentences that make sense
2. To learn word order in sentences
3. To develop an appreciation for the printed word
4. To develop visual discrimination skills
5. To develop problem-solving skills
6. To develop eye–hand coordination skills
7. To practice forming letters
8. To develop small-muscle coordination skills

RELATED CURRICULUM THEMES:

Sentences

Stories

Writing

Reading

Communication

Our World

DIRECTIONS:

1. Center the title Sentence Sense at the top of a large piece of manuscript chart paper. (*See photograph.*)
2. Under the title, print these directions: Read the words. Write a sentence that makes sense.
3. Leave a blank line. Then print the following:

   cake I like

   fun Dogs are

   David cakes bakes

   play Kittens to like

   fort a Aaron made

   cereal ate Lindsay
4. Cover the finished piece with clear Con-Tact paper or laminate it.

TOOLS AND ACCESSORIES:

- Watercolor markers
- Crayons
- Grease pencil
- Damp cloth/sponge

VARIATIONS AND EXTENSIONS:

Substitute the names of children in your class when preparing the chart.

SHORT SENTENCES

Short Sentences
Look at the pictures. Read
the words. Draw a line to
make a short sentence.

A dog.   spins.
A fish   wiggles.
A snake   bounces.
A ball   barks.
A top   swims.

DEVELOPMENTAL GOALS:

1. To choose the correct verb to form short sentences
2. To develop an appreciation for the printed word
3. To develop visual discrimination skills
4. To develop problem-solving skills
5. To develop eye–hand coordination skills

RELATED CURRICULUM THEMES:

Sentences   Communication   Words

Reading   Writing   Our World

DIRECTIONS:

1. Across the top of a piece of heavy manuscript paper, print the title Short Sentences. If lined paper is unavailable, draw lines on tagboard.

2. Under the title, print these directions: Look at the pictures. Read the words. Draw a line to make a short sentence.

3. Draw a picture of a dog, fish, snake, ball and top, down the left side of the paper.

4. Print the name of the object down the left side of the paper—A dog, A fish, A snake, A ball and A top.

5. Print the words spins, wiggles, bounces, barks and swims down the right side of the paper.

6. Draw a broken line from "A dog" to "barks."

7. Cover the finished piece with clear Con-Tact paper or laminate it.

TOOLS AND ACCESSORIES:

• Watercolor markers

• Crayons

• Grease pencil

• Damp cloth/sponge

VARIATIONS AND EXTENSIONS:

1. Use sentences related to the curriculum theme.

2. If developmentally appropriate, write longer sentences.

MORE SHORT SENTENCES

More Short Sentences
Look at the pictures. Read the words. Draw a line to make a short sentence.

A flower   meows.
A cat   hops.
A bee   hits.
A rabbit   grows.
A bat   ticks.
A clock   stings.

DEVELOPMENTAL GOALS.

1. To develop skills in forming short sentences
2. To develop an appreciation for the printed word
3. To develop visual discrimination skills
4. To develop problem-solving skills
5. To develop eye–hand coordination skills

RELATED CURRICULUM THEMES:

Sentences   Communication   Words

Reading   Writing   Our World

DIRECTIONS:

1. Across the top of a piece of heavy manuscript paper, print the title More Short Sentences. If lined paper is unavailable, draw lines on tagboard.

2. Under the title, print these directions: Look at the pictures. Read the words. Draw a line to make a short sentence.

3. Draw a picture of a flower, cat, bee, rabbit, bat, and clock down the left side of the paper

4. Print the words behind each object down the left side of the paper: A flower, A cat, A bee, A rabbit, A bat, and A clock.

5. Print the words meows, hops, hits, grows, ticks, and stings down the right side of the paper.

6. Draw a broken line from "a flower" to "grows".

7. Cover the finished piece with clear Con-Tact paper or laminate it.

TOOLS AND ACCESSORIES:

- Watercolor markers
- Crayons
- Grease pencil
- Damp cloth/sponge

VARIATIONS AND EXTENSIONS:

1. Use sentences related to the curriculum theme.

2. If developmentally appropriate, write longer sentences.

VERBS

Verbs

1. The dog is _____ . (barking - cooking)
2. The pig is _____ . (begging - digging)
3. The cow is _____ . (mooing - barking)
4. The kitten is _____ . (burring - purring)
5. The jet is _____ . (flying - singing)
6. The turtle is _____ . (crying - crawling)
7. The car is _____ . (moving - playing)

DEVELOPMENTAL GOALS:

1. To complete sentences by identifying the correct verb
2. To develop an appreciation for the printed word
3. To develop visual discrimination skills
4. To develop problem-solving skills
5. To develop eye–hand coordination skills
6. To practice forming letters
7. To develop small-muscle coordination skills

RELATED CURRICULUM THEMES:

Sentences   Communication   Words

Reading   Writing   Symbols

DIRECTIONS:

1. Across the top of a piece of heavy manuscript chart paper, print the title Verbs.
2. Under the title, print the following:

    The dog is —————— (barking–cooking).

    The pig is ————— (begging–digging).

    The cow is ————— (mooing–barking).

    The kitten is ————— (burring–purring).

    The jet is ————— (flying–singing).

    The turtle is ————— (crying–crawling).

    The car is ————— (moving–playing).

3. Cover the finished piece with clear Con-Tact paper or laminate it.

TOOLS AND ACCESSORIES:

- Watercolor markers
- Crayons
- Grease pencil
- Damp cloth/sponge

VARIATIONS AND EXTENSIONS:

1. Write sentences related to the curriculum theme.
2. If developmentally appropriate, write longer sentences.

MORE VERBS

More Verbs

1. The fish is _____ . (swim – swimming)
2. The boat is _____ . (moving – move)
3. The birds are _____ . (flying – fly)
4. The ball is _____ . (roll – rolling)
5. The girl is _____ . (play – playing)
6. Eric is _____ . (helping – help)
7. Nikita is _____ . (swing – swinging)
8. Diane is _____ . (work – working)

DEVELOPMENTAL GOALS:

1. To complete sentences with the correct verb form
2. To develop an appreciation for the printed word
3. To develop visual discrimination skills
4. To develop problem-solving skills
5. To develop eye–hand coordination skills
6. To practice forming letters
7. To develop small-muscle coordination skills

RELATED CURRICULUM THEMES:

Sentences   Communication   Words

Reading   Writing   Symbols

DIRECTIONS:

1. Across the top of a piece of heavy manuscript paper, print the title More Verbs.

2. Under the titles, print the following

   The fish is _____ (swim–swimming).

   The boat is _____ (move–moving).

   The birds are _____ (fly–flying).

   The ball is _____ (roll–rolling).

   Eric is _____ (help–helping).

   Nikita is _____ (swing–swinging).

   Diane is _____ (work–working).

3. Write the word that completes the sentence.

4. Cover the finished piece with clear Con-Tact paper or laminate.

TOOLS AND ACCESSORIES:

- Watercolor markers
- Crayons
- Grease pencil
- Damp cloth/sponge

VARIATIONS AND EXTENSIONS:

1. Write sentences related to the curriculum theme.

2. If developmentally appropriate, write longer sentences.

"WAS" AND "WERE"

"Was" and "Were"
Read each line. Write the word that completes the sentence.

1. Lori _____ riding.
   (was · were)
2. Lori and Lisa _____ riding.
   (was · were)
3. Hannah _____ singing.
   (was · were)
4. Hannah and Tim _____ singing.
   (was · were)
5. He _____ playing.
   (was · were)
6. They _____ playing.
   (was · were)

DEVELOPMENTAL GOALS:

1. To practice selecting the correct verb form
2. To develop an appreciation for the printed word
3. To develop visual discrimination skills
4. To develop problem-solving skills
5. To develop eye–hand coordination skills
6. To develop small-muscle coordination skills
7. To practice forming letters

RELATED CURRICULUM THEMES:

Sentences

Writing Tools

Writing

Our World

Communication

Symbols

DIRECTIONS:

1. Print the title "Was" and "Were" across the top of a large piece of manuscript chart paper. (*See photograph.*)
2. Under the title, print these directions: Read each line. Write the word that completes the sentence.
3. Leave a blank line. Then print the following:

    Lori _____ riding. (was–were)

    Lori and Lisa _____ riding. (was–were)

    Hannah _____ singing. (was–were)

    Hannah and Tim _____ singing. (was–were)

    He _____ playing. (was–were)

    They _____ playing. (was–were)

4. Cover the finished piece with clear Con-Tact paper or laminate it.

TOOLS AND ACCESSORIES:

- Watercolor markers
- Crayons
- Grease pencil
- Damp cloth/sponge

VARIATIONS AND EXTENSIONS:

1. Print the letter *a* or *e* on the lines to provide a clue for the children.
2. Use the names of children in your class in the sentences.

MORE "WAS" AND "WERE"

More "Was" and "Were"
Read each line. Write the
word that completes the
sentence.

1. The dog _____ eating.
   (was · were)
2. The dogs _____ eating.
   (was · were)
3. The men _____ walking.
   (was · were)
4. The man _____ walking.
   (was · were)
5. The babies _____ crying.
   (was · were)
6. The baby _____ crying.
   (was · were)

DEVELOPMENTAL GOALS:

1. To complete sentences with the correct verb form
2. To develop an appreciation for the printed word
3. To develop visual discrimination skills
4. To develop problem-solving skills
5. To develop eye–hand coordination skills
6. To develop small-muscle coordination skills
7. To practice forming letters

RELATED CURRICULUM THEMES:

Sentences

Writing Themes

Writing

Writing Tools

Communication

Symbols

DIRECTIONS:

1. Print the title More Was and Were across the top of a large piece of manuscript chart paper. (*See photograph.*)
2. Under the title, print these directions: Read each line. Write the word that completes the sentence.
3. Leave a blank line. Then print the following:

   1. The dog _____ eating. (was–were)
   2. The dogs _____ eating. (was–were)
   3. The men _____ walking. (was–were)
   4. The man _____ walking. (was–were)
   5. The babies _____ crying. (was–were)
   6. The baby _____ crying. (was–were)

4. Cover the finished piece with clear Con-Tact paper or laminate it.

TOOLS AND ACCESSORIES:

- Watercolor markers
- Crayons
- Grease pencil
- Damp cloth/sponge

VARIATIONS AND EXTENSIONS:

Print the letter *a* or *e* on the lines to provide a clue for the children.

WRITE SENTENCES

Write Sentences

Write a sentence about each picture.

DEVELOPMENTAL GOALS:

1. To practice writing sentences
2. To develop an appreciation for the printed word
3. To develop visual discrimination skills
4. To develop problem-solving skills
5. To develop eye–hand coordination skills
6. To develop small-muscle coordination skills

RELATED CURRICULUM THEMES:

Symbols

Writing Tools

Writing

Sentences

Communication

Our Alphabet

DIRECTIONS:

1. Select a colored piece of tagboard.
2. Cut five sentence strips.
3. Cut three pictures from magazines, books, or equipment catalogs.
4. Print the title Write Sentences on one sentence strip. Apply paste and center it at the top of the tagboard.(*See photograph.*)
5. On a second strip, print the following: Write a sentence about each picture.
6. Apply paste and center this strip under the title.
7. Paste one of the pictures three inches from the left margin. Next to the picture, paste a blank sentence strip. Repeat for the second and third picture.
8. Cover the finished piece with clear Con-Tact paper or laminate it.

TOOLS AND ACCESSORIES:

- Watercolor markers
- Crayons
- Grease pencil
- Damp cloth/sponge

VARIATIONS AND EXTENSIONS:

1. Pictures related to the current curriculum theme could be used.
2. Pictures taken in the classroom could be used.
3. The children can draw or cut out their own pictures for the piece.

WRITE A STORY

Write a Story
Read the sentences. They are out of order. Write the sentences to tell a story.

They saw an elephant.
Chris and Kelsi went to
    the zoo.
They went home after dark

DEVELOPMENTAL GOALS:

1. To use sentences to tell a story
2. To develop an appreciation for the printed word
3. To develop visual discrimination skills
4. To develop problem-solving skills
5. To develop eye–hand coordination skills
6. To develop small-muscle coordination skills
7. To practice forming letters

RELATED CURRICULUM THEMES:

Stories

Reading

Sentences

Writing

Communication

Our World

DIRECTIONS:

1. Print the title Write a Story across the top of a large piece of manuscript paper. (*See photograph.*)
2. Under the title, print these directions: Read the sentences. They are out of order. Arrange the sentences to tell a story.
3. Leave a blank line. Then print the following: They saw an elephant. Chris and Kelsi went to the zoo. They went home after dark.
4. Cover the finished piece with clear Con-Tact paper or laminate it.

TOOLS AND ACCESSORIES:

- Watercolor markers
- Crayons
- Grease pencil
- Damp cloth/sponge

VARIATIONS AND EXTENSIONS:

1. Create charts with similar sentences related to the curriculum theme.
2. Encourage children to create their own stories, and display them on the bulletin board.

WRITE ANOTHER STORY

Write Another Story
Read the sentences. They
are out of order. Write the
sentences to tell a story.

The tooth fairy gave her a
    quarter.
One day it fell out.
Sally's tooth was loose.
She put it under her pillow.

DEVELOPMENTAL GOALS:

1. To practice writing sentences to tell a story
2. To develop an appreciation for the printed word
3. To develop visual discrimination skills
4. To develop problem-solving skills
5. To develop eye–hand coordination skills
6. To develop small-muscle coordination skills
7. To practice forming letters

RELATED CURRICULUM THEMES:

Stories

Communication

Sentences

Reading

Our World

Writing

DIRECTIONS:

1. Print the title Write Another Story across the top of a large piece of manuscript paper. (*See photograph.*)
2. Under the title, print these directions: Read the sentences. They are out of order. Arrange the sentences to tell a story.
3. Leave a blank line. Then print the following: The tooth fairy gave her a quarter. One day it fell out. Sally's tooth was loose. She put it under her pillow.
4. Cover the finished piece with clear Con-Tact paper or laminate it.

TOOLS AND ACCESSORIES:

- Watercolor markers
- Crayons
- Grease pencil
- Damp cloth/sponge

VARIATIONS AND EXTENSIONS:

Create stories around people and experiences, such as:

- My friend
- Mother's Day
- My favorite person
- Fire fighters
- Mail carriers
- Hair stylists
- A trip to the apple orchard
- A trip to the dentist
- A trip to the circus
- Halloween
- Thanksgiving
- Valentine's Day

a

b

c

d

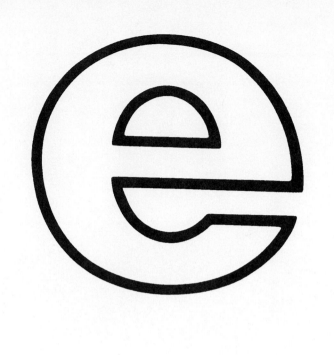

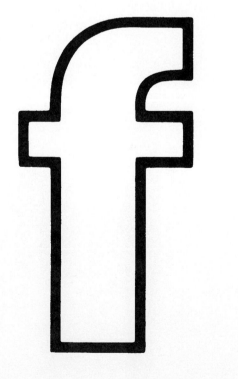

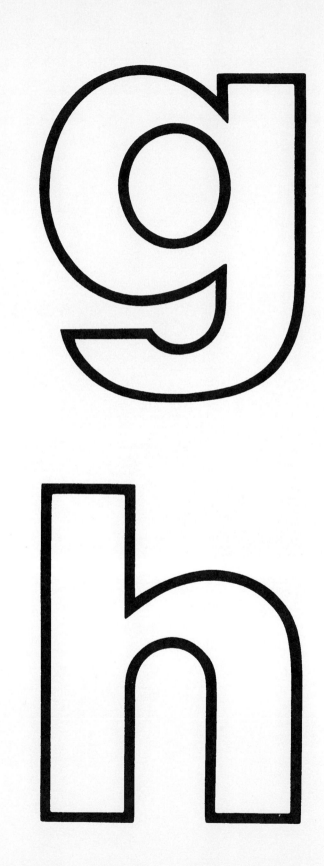

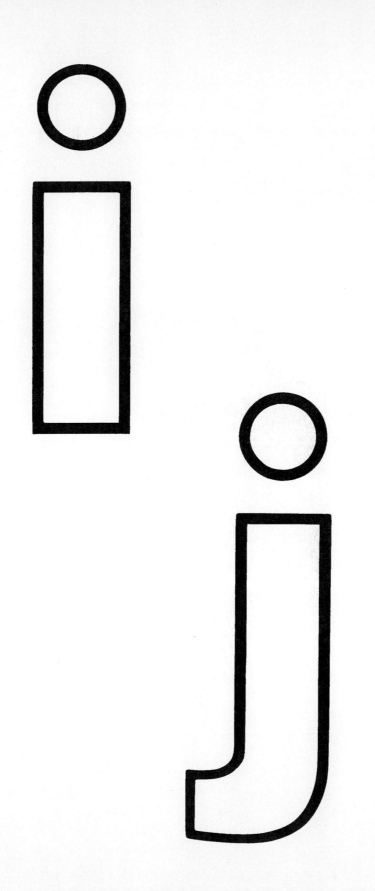

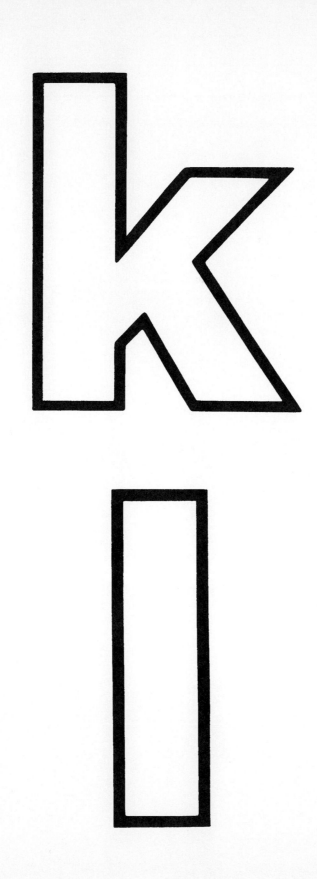

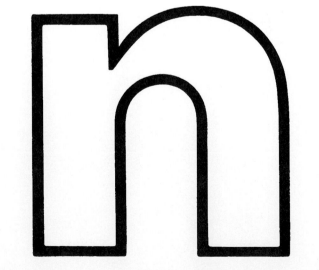

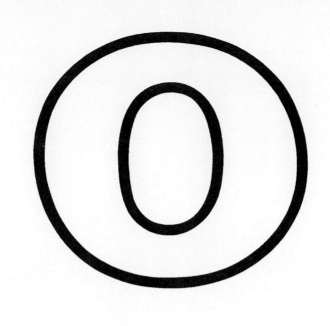

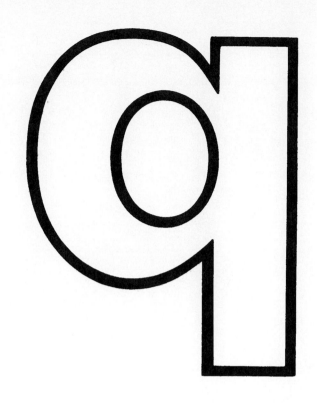

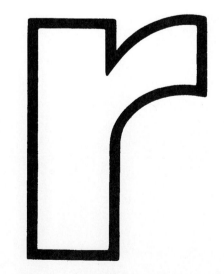

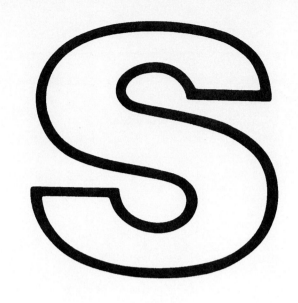

u

v

W

X

y

z

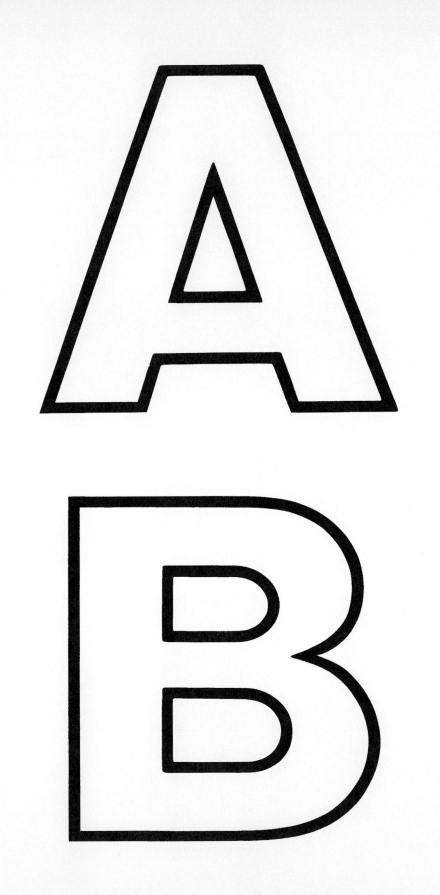

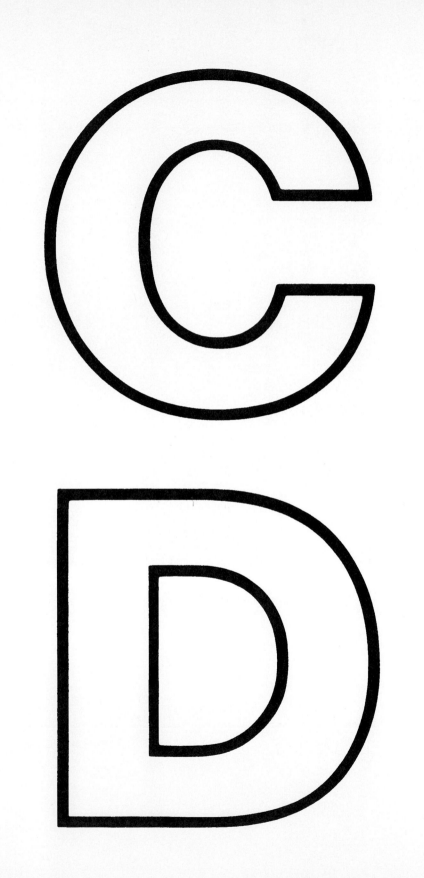

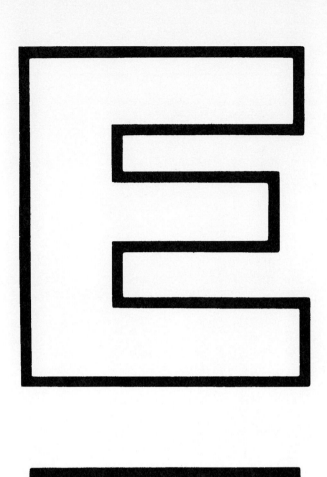

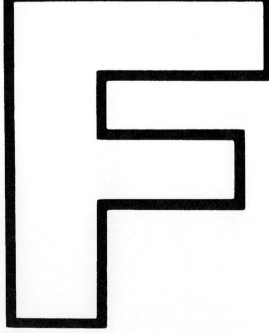

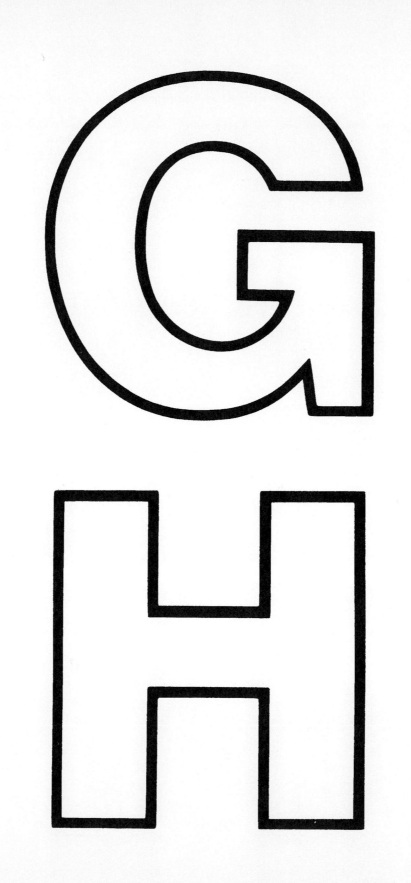

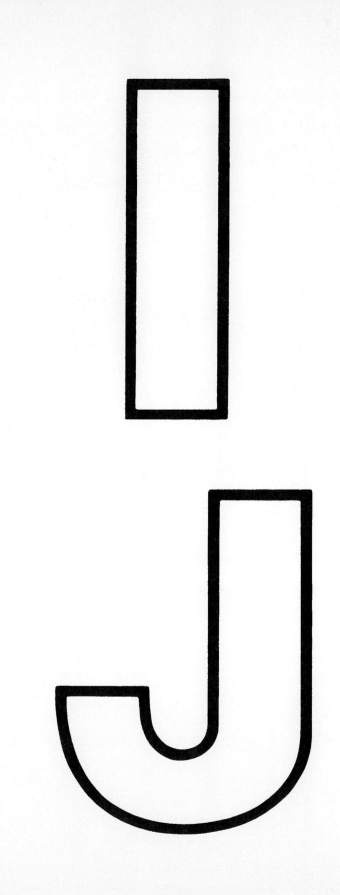

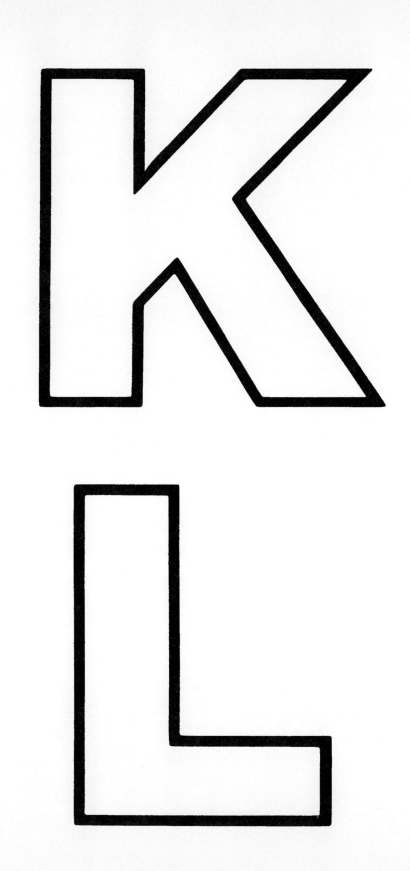

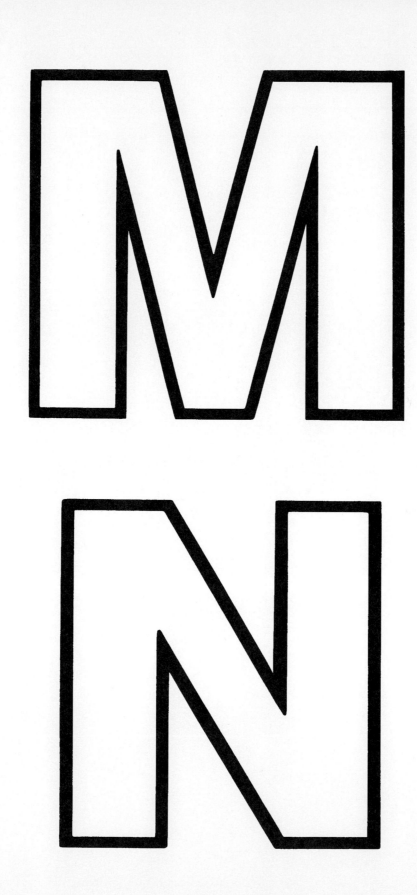

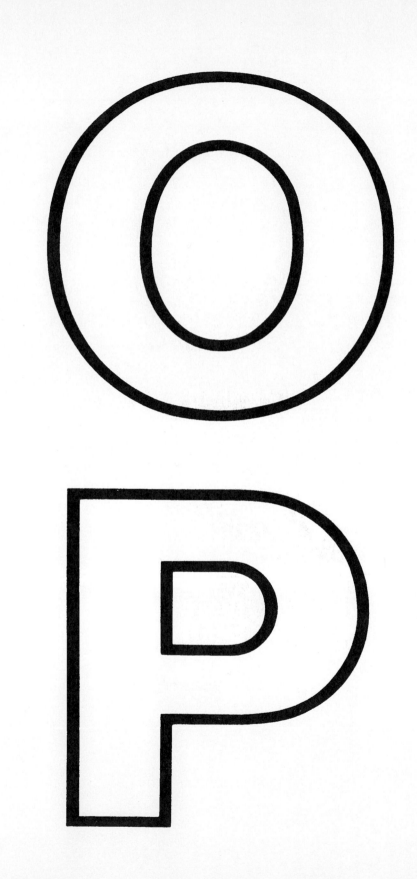

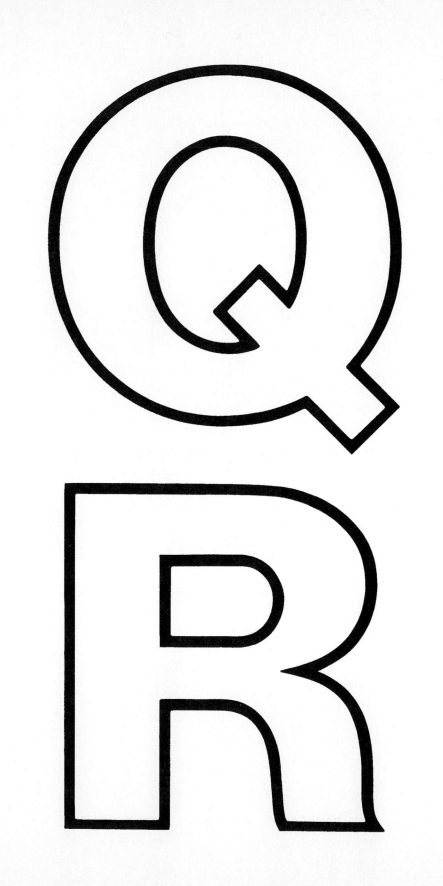

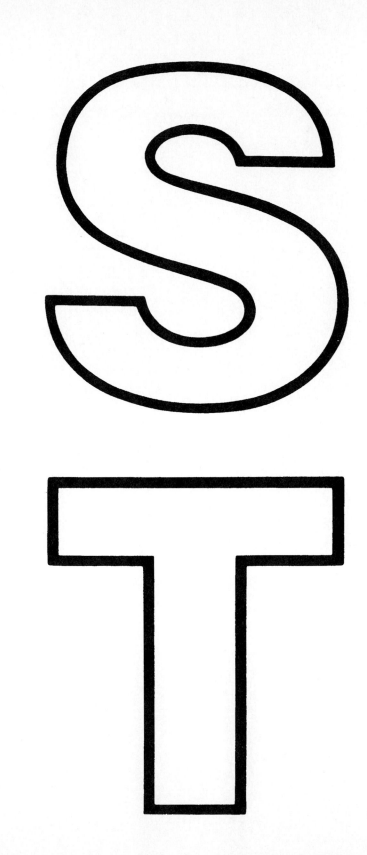

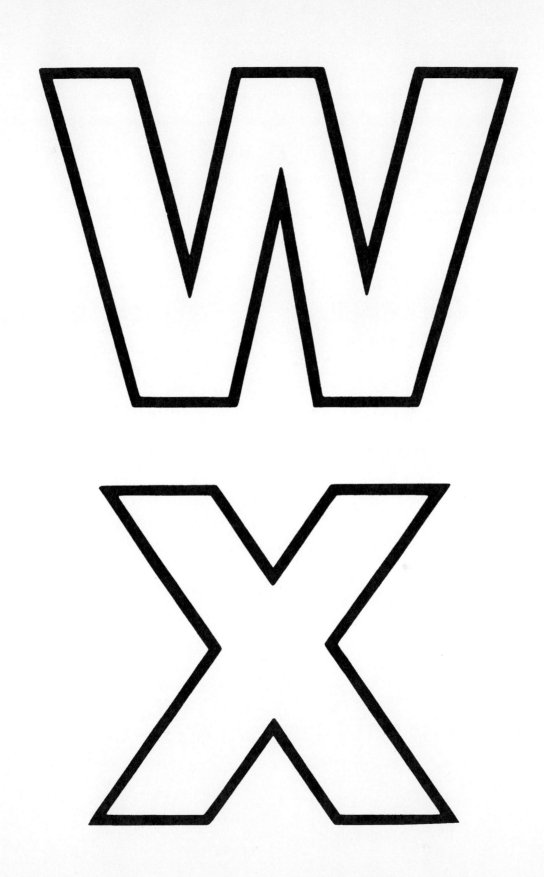

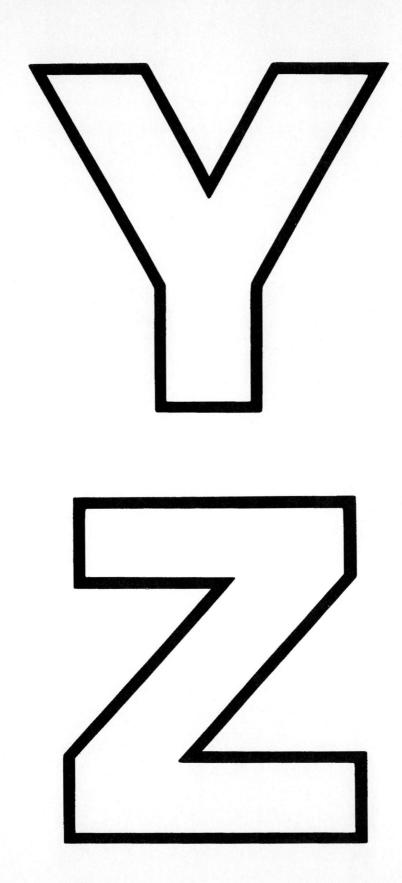

1

2

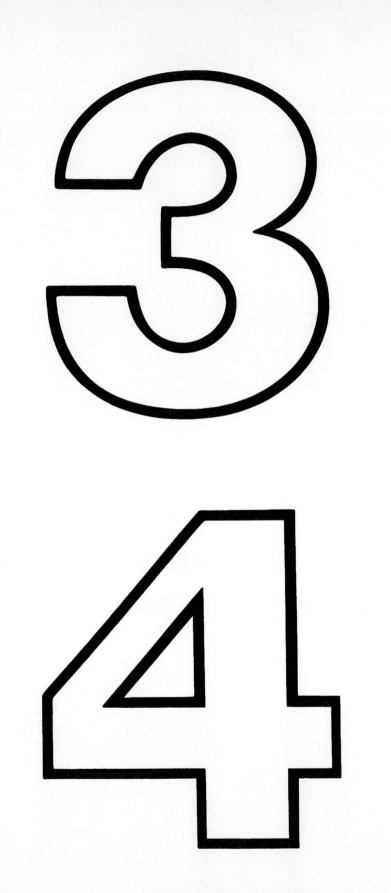

5

6

7

8

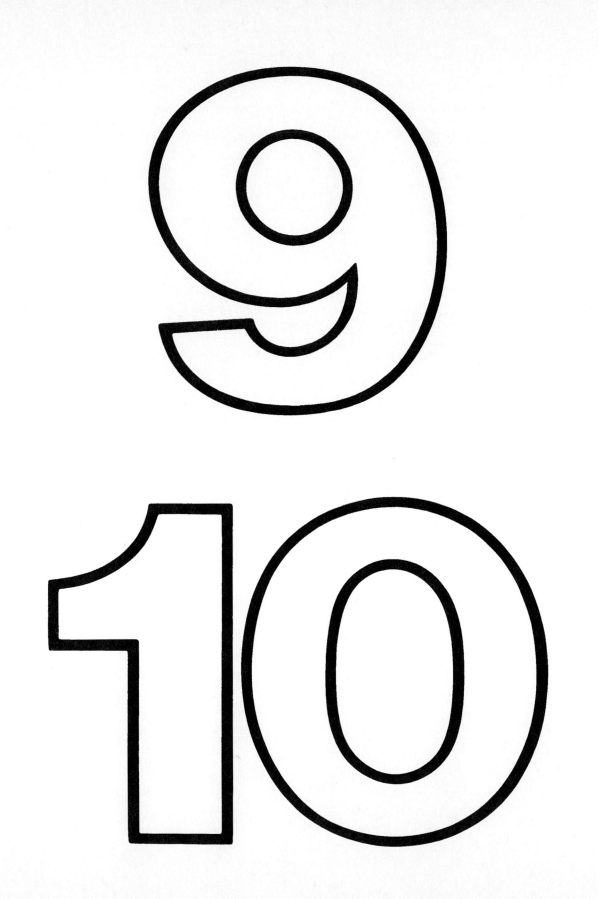